Insights

Mount St. Joseph Freshman English Anthology

Doug Lambdin   Dan Peightel   Erin Van Bavel

A Note to Our Students:

Freshman English at Mount St. Joseph encourages you to explore a wide variety of genres. The pieces collected here provide examples of where your exploration might take you. Whether working on a sonnet or a free verse poem, a memoir or a profile, a short story, a project proposal, or a professional email, every writer must make choices about subject, audience, and purpose. As working writers, we know the value of having models to emulate. Seeing how other writers have solved a particular writing problem can help you make your own choices. Some of the models in this collection come with keys to writing in a particular genre, explanations of the writer's choices, and suggestions for enhancing your style. Other models invite you to develop as a writer by considering a finished piece standing alone. Either way, we hope you will be inspired to tell your own stories.

Contents

Blood
By Doug Lambdin
Published in *Urbanite Magazine*
(memoir)

When the nurse technician's foot snagged and yanked the catheter tube leading up into my father's bladder, I heard him scream out for the first time in my life. His hands cupped tightly at his groin. We consoled him, failingly, while sneering at the tech. She only said, "You might see a little blood in the tube for a bit." And then she left.

He soon stopped squinting his eyes and clenching his teeth, and his breathing slowed. "Dear God!" he said. At eighty, he lay there looking as weak and vulnerable as a toddler, something I wasn't prepared for. But being a dad of a toddler myself, I instinctively wanted to take his pain, to put myself in that bed and be hooked up to all those wires and tubes, like some sort of human carburetor, and take his failing heart into my chest. And then he could comfort me, much like he did when I was four.

While playing a game of tag, Stephanie, from three doors down, slammed her front door on the tip of my index finger, practically severing it, as I reached in to tag her back. It was the first time I had ever seen my own blood. Everyone was yelling, especially me. Just arriving home, my father came and took one look at my finger and said, "You'll be fine. They'll patch that right up." A calm came over me. Even at four, I knew that if he said so then it would be so. And it was.

But that only seems to work from parent to child.

In his catheter tube, I saw his blood blending into his collected urine, turning it from gold to rust. My heart ached. Yet, I didn't say a word.

The point of the memoir:

A short memoir/essay should have a singular focus. However, it could have overlapping themes. For instance, the singular topic in the essay Blood is the effect of seeing the father in such a vulnerable state and being helpless to fix him, helpless to be able to repay what the father had so easily been able to do for the child. Yet, the themes are many: the roles of parent and child, the relationship between parent and child, mortality, trust. The "blood" of these moments are just vehicles to explore the themes our blood relationships.

Within the essay:
- Notice that the essay is broken into five parts: the opening scene in the hospital, a reflection/reaction to seeing the father in so vulnerable a position, an earlier childhood memory about bleeding, a reflection on that memory of how the father gave relief but how the child could not, back to beginning scene in the hospital room.

- There are two story memories that are bridged. The first takes place within the span of seconds, the catheter being yanked and then the blood appearing. The second, severing the fingertip and then at the ambulance, not much longer. The memoir/essay, however, is not just story. There is also reflection/reaction; the piece is a back and forth relationship between the two.

- Think about economy. If it's not needed, don't waste time giving it. Nowhere in the piece do I mention that it takes place in a hospital. Mentioning a nurse technician and a catheter will let the reader know where it is. Next, there is no date or day given. If it doesn't serve the piece, then it is not needed. Moreover, the affliction of the father is not even mentioned. It does not serve the piece, so it is not given. It is mentioned that the father is 80. The reader will deduce one of the many reasons an old person is in the hospital, but it would not change the effect of the piece.

Key elements when creating your memoir:

- Story and reflection/reaction. Give only what is needed in your story, and then react to it. It can be your reaction then and/or now. For example, the memory of the catheter being yanked and then the father's response. And then the reaction, the child looking at him and wanting to take his pain. He further reflects that he is not prepared to witness that yet, if ever.

- Later, there's the story of the tag game that results in a severed fingertip, and there is the reflection of how the father was able to calm the child, but the child cannot calm the father.

- Try to have a balance where you can. If there is too much story, then it will feel like a story. If there is too much reaction, the reader can lose what is being reacted to.

2. Begin at the moment of incident. There are many ways to begin a piece. This one starts with story, and it starts at the very moment of where the action begins, that inciting incident that ignites the cause and effect. (Back to economy again.) It doesn't start with the setting or day and place: "It was a gloomy Saturday morning at Baltimore General Hospital. My father, recovering from a prostate cancer procedure, lay in his bed...." Instead, this begins at the moment when the catheter is yanked. It will grab the reader's attention more, which is the point.

3. End back where you started. This is a stylistic suggestion. So many of us struggle with endings. Should I end with wisdom, a summary, perhaps a famous quote? They are a bit cliched, and they often fall flat. So, try to come full circle and put yourself back where you started. A full-circle ending. Psychologically, the reader will feel a sense of completeness, being back home again, back to the beginning. Often, just another bit of story at that place will lend itself to that analysis that the reader has already been giving the piece. This works well as a go-to because you have already created the place, so you do not have to work so hard to create something new, yet you will still be effective.

In this case, we are back looking at the catheter tube again. And the memory of not speaking supports the theme of helplessness. The silence speaks for itself.

Try it: To bolster your writing, try these other suggestions to elevate your style.

- Dramatic fragment: Try to use a fragment where you want to place extra emphasis on a particular moment. For example, "I was mortified. Devastated." It will jump off the page. In this piece, the fragment is an absolute phrase modifier, set apart from the sentence. "His hands cupped tightly at his groin."

- Modifiers: Use modifiers, whether at the beginning, middle, or at the end of sentences to combine information. For example: Participle phrase—"Just arriving home, my father came and took one look at my finger…"

- Single sentence/line paragraph: Look at your piece and pick a line that should stand apart from the rest, and make it its own paragraph. Try to keep it short and choppy. For example: "But that only seems to work from parent to child." This is the ah-ha moment of the piece; it demands its own paragraph.

- Title from within: Some writers start with a title. I almost never do that. If a great title came to me first, then I would; otherwise, I do not waste time creating one before I write. BUT, once the piece is done, look through it to find a word or phrase that would make a good title, and bring it to the top. Again, you are not working so hard trying to compose, but you can still be very effective. "Blood" works really well here because of the physical blood and the blood relations. However, "Gold to Rust" would work just as well: something valuable and precious like gold and life, juxtaposed with something we want to avoid like rust and death.

Under, Qualified
By Doug Lambdin
Published in *Smile, Hon. You're in Baltimore*
(short fiction)

Jordan stood on the front porch of the house, holding a colorful bouquet of mixed flowers in one arm, and staring at the sawed-off hammer that had been fashioned into a makeshift door knocker. He had half expected to see big Greek letters in the adjacent windows, as there were three other houses on the street with them, but there were none. He had been waiting in his car for several minutes, waiting for the last bit of sunlight to disappear, waiting until it was officially dark. He never wanted to enter with the sun behind him. And now standing on the porch, he paused, glad no one was following him in.

From inside, he could hear the loud mingle of voices and the rapid pulse of a speaker's bass. Jordan began his pre-party ritual: he turned his cap around, checked the fly on his jeans, popped in a fresh stick of spearmint gum and began chewing; and as he chewed he chanted: "Fun and funny. Fun and funny. Fun and funny." All he had to do was be himself; he wasn't being paid for anything beyond that. But there was a tacit expectation of more, so he always treated these parties like a role, as a professional would.

The autumn air felt good, and he could smell that someone had a fire going, maybe there. He almost wished that he could linger there a little longer, perhaps on the bench swing to the right, rocking ever so slightly back and forth in the breeze.

But there was work to be done.

Jordan couldn't reach the hammer-knocker even on tip-toes. No matter. He never knocked unless instructed; that's not how you enter a party if someone's paying you to bring the party. Instead, he gripped the round door knob, his fingers barely stretching over the edges, turned it, and charged right in, closing the door behind him. Immediately, Jordan saw people down the hall in the kitchen, and there were people in the living room to his right, just off the foyer. Behind all the chatter, he could hear bottles clinking, and someone was smoking a cigar. He strutted into the living room, wedging between a few folks who looked behind themselves and then down as he passed. He stopped at a tiny clearing next to the coffee table. He lifted his free into the air making a backwards peace sign and shouted, "What uuuuuup!" He froze for a moment in that pose, and then followed, "Where's the birthday girl?"

Everyone in the room was staring down at him. Jordan actually liked this moment, his entrance in the center ring. Mouths agape. Eyes fixed and bulging. "What're you people looking at?" He asked. "Haven't you ever seen a bouquet of flowers before?" Mouths began to close.

From the kitchen and through the dining room behind the living room came a man dividing everyone in his way. He wore a blue plaid flannel shirt that hung out untucked over slouchy blue jeans. He wore his black cap backwards, but Jordan quickly made out the small black bird's head with a purple B in the middle, above the man's forehead. In one hand was a can of National Bohemian beer. As he neared Jordan, he reached out his free hand and spouted, "Jordayyyyy! Waz up, dog," he said as he grabbed Jordan's hand. Jordan could feel the man's awkward attempt to shake hands, thumb around thumb, palm to palm. In his case, it just didn't work, so the man bent over and pulled Jordan in to hug it out.

"Dude! You're here!"

"I'm here."

"Everybody, this is Jordy...Jordy, this is everybody."

Actually, Jordan didn't like 'Jordy' at all. It was like a stage name, something to use at functions like these. 'Jordy' seemed much more fun than Jordan. Jordy brings the fun. Jordan sits home on weekends watching zombies and time lords. Yet, when he auditioned for an acting part, or even for being an extra, it was always Jordan, never Jordy.

The man spun around, calling out, "Kiiimm! Where's Kim!"

From the kitchen, above the din, a voice answered, "Comin'!" Now parting the crowd was a young woman, wearing tight blue jeans and a long sleeved, black tee shirt, perhaps more ballet top than tee shirt. She also wore a hat similar to the man's, but with her long, black ponytail pulled through the back. As she reached the man, her eyes fell on Jordan, and she stopped in her tracks.

"No! Way!" Kim spouted as she raised her hand to

her mouth.

"Happy birthday, baby" the man said, with a gentleness in his voice that implied that he recognized the gravity of such a sentimental moment.

And then she pointed at Jordan. "That is awesome."

Jordan walked to her, handed her the bouquet, and tugged on her arm to pull her down for a kiss. He stretched up toward her cheek, but at the last second, Kim wrapped her arms around Jordan and scooped him up, just as she would a Christmas puppy, and spun around, declaring, "I love it! I love it!"

Jordy was used to being lifted and spun, like a toddler, but without mom yelling, "WHEEEEEEEE!" Yet, he would wonder sometimes if people ever realized that they referred to him using pronouns for things—that, it. Kim planted Jordan back on the ground, but by then phones were already out, pictures already snapped, and within seconds thumbs were punching away at tiny screens.

Kim wrapped her arms around the man and declared, "Trey, you're the best. You know me like nobody else." She turned to Jordan, "Let's get a picture." She pulled a nearby barstool over and Trey hoisted Jordan up on to it, without checking first to see if Jordan could lift himself up onto it. He could. Yes, it would require some real maneuvering, but that's what the life was, some real maneuvering. But because he was being paid, people often took liberties with personal boundaries, pawing, grabbing, scooping, as though he were more teddy bear than man.

Kim and Trey lean their faces in close to Jordan's and they all smile, and Kim snaps a photo with the phone in her outstretched hand. Kim then turns toward Jordan and plants a kiss on his cheek, all the while stretching her eyes toward the phone. Jordan throws up a backward peace sign and makes a quick duck-face, and Kim snaps another pic.

"Ohmygod!" Kim said. "I don't know your name."

Before Jordan could respond, Trey interjected, "Jordaaayy!"

"Hey, Jordy. Do you need a beer?"

"Yeah," Trey said, "Get him a brew." Trey extended a hand to Jordan, "Dude, here, have a cigar."

Jordan didn't really smoke, but it was uncanny how many times he was given a cigar. He would always want to ask, So, where's the baby? He did know that people thought he looked funnier with a cigar, like a naughty little boy sneaking one of dad's Robustos, the stem barely fitting between his fingers. The natural one-liners about stunting his growth at the ready.

Jordan took the cigar, leaned into Trey's lighter, and pulled the flame into his cigar. With a glowing ember on the end of the cigar, he flipped his head back chomped down on the cigar, and scrunched his face up, with one eye open, like a two-bit gangster. Keep playing the part. That's what they are paying for. Jordy. There was even a little cheer from a couple of guys, as though this was his first cigar, and he was now in the fraternity.

And for the next hour and a half, that was how the

evening went, playing the part that he knew better than any of them. Kim and others got their picture with Jordan on their shoulders; Kim even got a pic of herself on Jordan's shoulders. He knew to nurse his beer, because as soon as his red cup looked near half empty, someone would grab it, just take it from him, and fill it back up.

"Let me top you off, little man." And inevitably, around this time someone would ask, "What should we call you? Not like, you know, m—" And they would leave their lips together making an M so they wouldn't actually say 'midget,' but imply the "M" word.

"I am what I am, man. Little person." But he would look up at them and wonder, Don't you watch cable? We're all over the place. How could you not know to call us 'little people,' butt-head! But tonight, there was a new role added to his repertoire. Trey and two of his cronies were playing beer pong on the dining room table, when Jordan heard erupt, "Dude, dude, dude, I got it. This'll be awesome." Jordan could see Trey swinging around the corner of the table with their eyes locked in on each other. Trey was waving him in with each step across the bare wood floor. Trey tugged on Jordan's sleeve demanding, "Dude, you gotta do this. This'll be awesome."

Jordan was sharing the smile on Trey's face. He seemed so happy with his idea. Jordan certainly didn't want to ruin the moment.

Trey escorted Jordan back to the dining room table, and then positioned Jordy about two feet from the edge. His chest just level with the table. Trey reached over and grabbed a beer mug, shook out any remaining drops onto the floor, and balanced it on Jordan's nearly bald head. And he beckoned to his buddies.

"Looklooklooklook...Beer Pong target."

From the others, Jordan could hear spouts of laughter, mixed with a few Ohmygod's and Dude, you're insane. A few girls nearby looked at him with their hands to their mouths.

Jordan had suffered these scenarios before: too much alcohol, and throw a little person in the mix. This is where Jordan made a commitment a long time ago. Sure, he could hop on a chair, smash the mug against the wall, and preach humanity to this drunkard's mass; but instead he followed his mantra that he didn't even have to chant to himself anymore—keep playing the part. Fun and funny. Fun and funny. Fun and funny.

Jordan grinned, lifted his shoulders, and threw his hands up in a gesture of good sportsmanship; and then he beckoned to Trey and his pals, daring them to try to make it.

Their aim was off, and they pelted Jordan everywhere but the glass. Jordan slowly spun around, gently swaying, as a taunt. But his real intention was to stop getting hit in the face. With his back to Trey, he crossed his arms and pulled an expression of boredom, even yawning. He looked at the crowd before him, who seemed to be giving him plenty of space. When there, across the room, leaning on the wall by a mantle of beer mugs, stood Lisa Sinclair. Lisa Sinclair. And Jordan saw she was looking back at him. Into his eyes.

Jordan resisted the temptation to swipe the glass from his head. He wouldn't dare wave. And he couldn't act as though he hadn't seen her; although he wished he could. So, he began turning back around. Face to face with Trey again, Jordan took a Ping-Pong ball to the forehead. He pulled the glass down and placed it on the table between them.

"Duuuude!" one of Trey's friends complained.

"I gotta go to the bathroom," Jordan answered." "You guys weren't gonna sink one anytime this year anyway."

"Harsh, bro."

Jordan made his way upstairs to the bathroom, not once looking in Lisa Sinclair's direction. Lisa Sinclair, the one girl who Jordan, whenever he lapsed into a dark reverie about his high school days, remembered as kind. She sat next to him in Government and in Spanish 2. They even worked together on their final census project, for which Jordan created all the illustrations. It was her encouragement that made him believe he could be an artist. "Jordan," she would say, "one day I'm gonna be walking through an art gallery looking at beautiful pictures, and in the corners I'll see your name."

However, the closest he ever came to that gallery was creating an illustration for the back of a fundraiser's pamphlet for the local animal rescue. A pit bull looking overly bored at a calico cat on its back, pawing a felt bird. There was too much competition in a field where advancement came from distinguishing yourself or having the right mix of talent and connections. Jordan, like most others, had none of those. But, he felt he could distinguish himself, somehow.

At the bathroom sink, Jordan was scouring his hands, as though he could scrub away time, at least the last three years at Dwarves on Demand. Even further, he would go back to that moment right after high school, when anything and everything was possible, just like the counselors said. Back to that summer air that was sweet and light because it was the first breath for all the great things he was destined to do. If only I could open this door and step back into that moment, true or not, Jordan thought. He toweled his hands and opened the door. Lisa Sinclair was standing at the doorway.

"Hi, Jordan," she said. Her hair was shorter now, and straighter. But she still smelled of perfume and spearmint gum. God! Jordan was instantly reminded how much he loved that blend. He had forgotten that he used to hope that whoever he married would smell just like that. It would be a bonus, he'd fantasize, if she would have that same full bottom lip. Lisa Sinclair was as still as beautiful. More.

"Heyyyy, Lisa, I thought that was you. Great to see you again. You look great. What's happening?" Okay, shut up, Jordan thought. Listen and nod and move on. He was squeezing past her, his back now to the stairs, showing that he was en route and couldn't talk long.

"Jordan, I didn't know you knew Trey and Kim."

"Yeah, yeah, well not well, but yeah, yeah. So what's happening with you?"

"Jordan, were you hired tonight?"

"Huh, yeah well this is what I do. It's awesome, right? I get paid to hang out at parties and drink beer and eat. I bring the fun. Awesome, right? You know what I mean? So what are you doing these days?" Jordan took a step back.

"You were going to be an artist."

"Oh, I am. Y'know, starving artist. I've done a couple things, but I'm branching out, getting into acting. Livin' the dream. It's all good. How about you? You gotta be runnin' the world soon, right?"

"I'm back in school."

"Yeah, you were always the smart one." Jordan was standing near the edge of the steps; he would either dive into her arms or bolt down the steps, but he had to make a big move any moment or he would boil then and there. He hated how she was looking at him. Not down at him but into him. And not with pity, but with disappointment. Who the hell are you," he screamed in his head.

"So were you."

Jordan slipped down the step and grabbed onto the railing. "Whoa, no more for me. Perks of the job. I gotta get back. I'd love to catch up. Wow, Lisa Sinclair! You on Facebook? I'll definitely look for you." Jordan bounded down the steps and into the kitchen. No one was there. Everyone had diverged at once. But that would only last a moment, Jordan reasoned. He suddenly felt panicked. He stepped toward the dining room, but then paused. He pivoted, looked at the clock above the sink. Ten o' seven. Off the clock. Jordan slid out the back door.

The night air was good and cold, and the sudden silence was a balm. He knew that no one would miss him at this point. He had served his purpose. And tomorrow when they were sober, they would actually remember saying goodbye.

Back in his car, Jordan sat with the music off but the heater on, staring up at the front door of the house. He imagined Lisa Sinclair stepping through the door and to the edge of the porch. Her arms crossed and her shoulders raised, bracing against the chill, looking right and then left, and then again.

Jordan pulled out his cell phone and scrolled through the calendar. Next week he was booked for a party off of Loch Raven Boulevard. Who, he wondered, would Lisa Sinclair know there?

Point: This story grew out of the challenge to try and write a story from a perspective other than my own, one with which I am unfamiliar.

Keys:
- Obviously, pick a perspective that is not similar to your own.

- This is realistic fiction, meaning that it feels as though it could actually happen. So, the story should seem as though it could actually happen.

- Use a mix of dialogue, narration, and reflection, not just one.

Try it:
- Only give needed dialogue, meaning do not give dialogue if it does not serve the scene.

- Write dialogue here and there as a character would speak it. This story takes place in Baltimore, so dropping a 'g' at the end of a word here and there shows that. Moreover, try some dialogue fragments. We do not always speak in complete sentences.

- Show not tell: Do not write a descriptive word when you could show it and make the reader think it.

Tilt

By Doug Lambdin

First Place Fiction Winner for Towson University's
Homeland's Three Arts Prize

Previously Published in *The Baltimore Review*

(short fiction)

Miles and I were the exact same height, probably to
the millimeter, but he always insisted he was half an inch
taller. It didn't bother me too much; all of the men in my
family were over six feet tall. Even a few women were an
eyelash short of the big six. But there wasn't a soul alive
or dead related to miles who was over five feet nine and
one-half inches. In my house we walked among giants
and he knew I would join them one day. He also knew
that my father was a pacifist, though he swore his dad
could beat up my dad, "...if it ever came down to it."

Miles and I were best friends, or rather I was his
best friend. I didn't have many of my own and he paid me
the most mind. I had a lot of friendship to give and he
required a lot. When we first met during a pack meeting
in cub scouts, he threatened to beat me up.   He was
impressed by a sleight-of-hand magic trick I knew. I made
a thimble on the end of my index finger disappear in the
palm of my other hand and then reappear behind it. He
hated that he couldn't figure it out, so he wanted to beat
me up. I wasn't afraid though maybe I should've been.
He grew to have a reputation as the toughest fighter
around. I just dismissed him with a wave of disinterest,
which perplexed and infuriated him. But he didn't act. He

just persisted with threats and I taught him the trick. He never mastered it. From then on we were known as "The Terrible Duo." At least in certain circles. Actually, he did most of the "terrible." I was just "terrible" by association. Regardless, we were inseparable, to his credit.

I admit, I was very impressed by Miles since our first meeting in Pack 564. He wasn't afraid of anything or anyone and I was jealous of that. Actually that's not entirely true, I think Miles was afraid of the game ending and he's be left being "it." I think this haunted him. The solution was to never end the game.

By the time we reached Junior High we pledged a thousand times that we would always be friends. No matter whom we married or how many times, we would always live near each other and our kids would play together. We knew it was odd to be thinking about marriage and kids at such an age, but certainly no girl would come between us. None ever did. Girls interested us but they weren't essential to our dream. It was the woods that we loved, equally.

Neither of us loved the woods more than the other, and there was no jealousy. When we wanted adventure, we went to the woods. When we wanted to get away, we went to the woods. When we wanted to be like men, the woods let us be men. At fourteen, we didn't know many of the unanswerable questions yet, but there were answers in the woods. And so early on both days of every weekend I pedaled four miles on my Schwinn Mongoose to Miles' house. I had a knapsack, and I always brought the corn chips and Tastykakes. Miles always supplied the subs and Cokes. And of course, treats for Tilt.

Tilt was Miles' charcoal Keeshond. He was a medium-sized dog with a thick coat of long, straight hair; and he had a foxlike head with small, pointed ears and a tail that curled over his back. He was devoted to Miles. His eyes were colored deep brown with understanding. When he was a puppy, Miles' father won him playing pinball while stationed in Saudi Arabia. On his next visit home, he brought Tilt back as a present for Miles. Usually he brought back sneakers or appliances.

Whenever we went out on an excursion, I carried the pack and Miles was in charge of the weaponry. Two Christmases previous he had received an air-powered Daisy Pellet and B-B Rifle complete with scope. A year later he saved and bought a Daisy Air Pump Pellet and B-B Pistol, which was I generally used. One cloudy and damp April Sunday morning he requested that I grab the guns from the cellar to carry while he would carry the pack. I was honored.

Side by side the three of us descended the hill behind his development and headed for our haunts. We had a strict routine, which went as follows: we stash the sack at the fort, and then cross the creek to a heavily knotted rope swing for true jungle activity, followed by target practice at the bottom of an uprooted elm. The targets du jour were some flash cubes Miles took from his mother's camera, which she never used, and a can of Right Guard deodorant I swiped form my father, of which he used too much. About a half mile deep into the woods, but about a hundred yards before the rope swing, lay the thickest patch of evergreens in the entire area. Centered in the trees was a small clearing that housed a hollowed out briar bush dome. In the base of the far side was a small tunnel that allowed us to enter only on hands and knees. Tilt was already inside, and Miles followed to shed the weight of his pack, but he didn't come out.

"Aren't you comin' in?"

"Why should I, aren't we headin' out?"

"Nah, let's hang out awhile."

"Hang out?"

"Just get in here."

I crawled in on 1X6's we had put down the previous Fall. Once inside I stood and walked six paces to the far side and placed the guns on one of the picnic benches in the living quarters. We had marked off a living room consisting of two benches and a dining area with the third. We even had a library, which was really nothing more than an old metal box that used to be kept on a porch for the milk man to drop off his delivery. It held our treasure stock of Mad and National Lampoon. But the jewel in the crown was a magazine with a missing cover Miles found in a dumpster.   It was filled with nothing but large-breasted women with shiny black hair.

I turned around. "All right---," but Miles was bent over coughing. However, his right arm was extended out toward me as far as he could stretch it and in his hand was a bottle with the cap off. He stood with a red face, puffy eyes, and wet lips under his blonde hair.

"You alright?"

"Yeah, 'ere."

"What?"

"Take it. I swiped it from outta the closet in the basement." Miles "swiped" everything in his life. His father was only in town twice a year for no more than two weeks at a time. But when he was, Miles swiped every stray bill and disregarded coin his father left on the dresser, nightstand, or coffee table, like he was gathering nuts for the winter. His father never said a word. Once Miles took two hundred dollars out of his father's billfold and it was never missed.

His mother, on the other hand, was home almost always. But she might as well not have been there at all. She sat in her room most of the time smoking. There was an actual light brown soot stain on the ceiling above her bed. She would venture out only to the kitchen and the bathroom. She rarely went anywhere except to the supermarket, which was twice a month, but when she did Miles drove.

"You gotta be kiddin'."

"I thought we'd start off with a little of brunch of champions."

"I've never…"

"Well there you go."

"I don't…I…"

"C'monnn, don't be a wuss."

Timing was everything to Miles. He never jeopardized a moment with build-up. Spontaneity was his best attack. Never give your opponent time to think. I took the bottle in my hand a put it to my nose.

"Oh my God! This smells like something my mother

would clean the toilet with. There's no way if I drink this I won't RALPH all over the place."

"Here." Miles reached into the pack. Take a little drink and then munch these.

"But won't your mother—"

"By the time we get home my mom will be in her room for the night."

I put the bottle to my lips, pressing hard.

"Whoa! You alright, here quick eat, eat."

"Cough—"

"Okay?"

"Ye…cough… yeah yeah yeah I'm good. Here gimme another handful…whew! Tilt was barking and weaving back and forth between us pogoing up and down with his front paws.

"That was beautiful. Next one'll be easier."

"I'm not goin' through that again."

"C'mon, it'll take the edge off."

"What edge?"

"I don't know." Miles shrugged and labored down another gulp.

"Backatcha."

"Gimme more chips."

Miles handed me the bottle and kept his arm extended, staring up, posing like Johnny Unitas on a football card. Tilt lay down on a small rug remnant we had brought in the first day of spring. An hour must've passed before we sat involuntarily. Within two hours we had had enough. The corn chips were gone and we had broken into the subs. It wasn't even noon and the bottle was half-empty. Even my grandmother didn't have her first martini before two. We made one final toast. "To Ollld Kentucky."

"Hear, hear…may her amber waves of grain…blow purple magic mountain…something, something, I don't know, whatever." Miles hid the bottle in the library under the trash bag. He stumbled to his knees and knelt there frozen looking seriously at the ground. Tilt came over and started licking his face. "Hello, puppyyy. Hello, pup." When he spoke little crumbs were flying out of his mouth, and Tilt went back to lie down. Miles fell forward still trying to pet him and caught himself and held there on all fours looking down, "Com'ere, puppy…"

"Dude man, I don't feel so hot."

Miles was laughing so hard he stopped making any sound. Tears and drool were forming tiny puddles on the ground.

"I gotta get outta here. I gotta get up and walk. I'm goin' out."

As soon as I started crawling out, Tilt was nipping at my heels to pass. I stood up with the help of a stump and staggered down a nearby path toward the creek. When I got to the edge, I stopped and teetered in place with my feet sinking in the moist earth. I threw up with the current, which left me feeling like I had been kicked in the groin.

The water was cold on my arms and knees but refreshing. I put my face under and washed out my mouth. I crawled to the grass and sat on the earth leaning back on a log. I tried to lie down but couldn't. After a long while Miles found me and collapsed a few feet away with the top of his head facing me. He had the guns with him and Tilt, who began lapping up the creek.

Miles arched his head back and rolled his eyes back to me, "You don't look so hot."

"Yeah, but I feel fresh as a...a lily."

"Did you go swimming?"

"I just needed a little water."

"Beautiful."

"That I am."

Miles stood up and fooled with Tilt's fur. "Don't move."

"It's so quiet—"

"Sit."

"Look at the tops of the trees sway—"

"You need a good brushing—

"The sky looks flat behind the trees—"

"I'm gonna have to cut this one out—"

"Whatta you wanna do?"

"We're doin' it."

We held our position for the next couple of hours, speaking briefly and in small sentences. And then Miles became very inquisitive. "Do you think I'll be ugly when I grow up?"

"Guaranteed."

"No really."

"I don't know, man. Why should you?"

"I don't know." He picked up a twig and started peeling the tip with his thumbnail. "If you ever had a million bucks and bought a huge mansion, would you let me live in it?"

You could have your own wing."

"Would you really do that?"

"Wouldn't you?"

"Of course."

"There you go then."

"That's cool. Do you ever think I'll get a girlfriend…a pretty one?"

"I don't know. I guess there's a girl out there for you. Can't imagine who."

"I hope she has nice feet."

"You and that damned "feet thing."

"You think I'll have ugly kids—"

"Would you shuuuuut uuuuuup!"

"Just askin'." Miles struggled to his feet but stayed a little bent over with his hands on his thighs, "I think I can walk."

"You wanna head back?"

"Nonono, let's head over and take in a little target practice."

"Oh, I couldn't hit the sky right now."

"We gotta then, it'll be hilarious."

"Right." When we reached the uprooted elm, I realized we hadn't brought our targets, so we settled for the roots jutting out from the stump. Neither of us was hitting a thing and soon I got tired of pumping my pistol. Tilt had moved far to our right to be out of harm's way. I dropped my arms and stared at the network of roots to see Miles' next shot, but he wasn't shooting. I looked over and Miles wasn't aiming at the tree. He was pointing his rifle to his right and looking through his scope positioning it, pinpointing his target. He was aiming right at Tilt and Tilt stood still as stone with his ears pricked in anticipation. *Miles fired!*

Tilt ran straight back to Miles on three legs, yelping all the way like a child running to his mother.

"Did you just shoot Tilt?"

Miles and met his dog. Tilt was holding his front paw out for inspection.

"You shot your dog, man! You shot Tilt—"

"He's not hurt—"

"How could you shoot your own dog; it's insane, man, look at him he ran right to you he trusts you and you shot him—"

"You're okay aren't you puppy yes you are you know I didn't mean it."

Miles was massaging his paw but Tilt was looking up at me.

I knew just how he felt. Once two summers before we were playing ball on a lot near Miles' house and Miles was tossing balls in the air and smacking them with his bat trying to hit me. I couldn't have been more than fifteen or twenty feet away. He hit me square in the gut and I lost my breath. I was crying and began to walk home and he dropped his bat and followed me begging me not to go saying he didn't mean it. He stood in my way and wouldn't let me pass. And said I could punch him in the stomach if I wanted. After a moment, I laughed and all was well. Yeah, I knew exactly how he felt. I don't know which of us was more loyal or more stupid.

Within a minute Tilt was walking fine, and all was well.

"Didn't even break the skin."

"You shot your own dog!"

"I only gave it one pump. I knew it wouldn't hurt him."

"You could've shot his eye out! Or maybe killed him!"

"I wasn't aiming anywhere near his head."

"Oh well that makes it okay."

"Why are you I' so worked up? I was only jokin'."

"You hear that Tilt he was only jokin' yeah that's better he understands now."

He just shook his head, put his rIfle on his shoulder, and started for home. He slapped his thigh a couple of times. "Tilt!"

We walked home silent and in single file, never stopping back at the fort for our gear or the Tastykakes. When we got back we ate again and went to bed. It was five in the afternoon. We slept until ten the next morning, or rather I slept until ten the next morning. Miles spent most of the night hunched over the toilet.

We never spoke of the incident again. Two weeks later Tilt was stolen, or maybe he had enough and ran away. Two weeks later, I ran away.

Point: Create a piece of realistic fiction that is dialogue driven.

Keys:

- Dialogue. Include dialogue, but avoid dialogue that's not needed. If it doesn't serve the scene, don't include it. Don't start with "Hey, what's up?" If it's not needed. Jump to the dialogue that drives the story.

- Include dialogue that's realistic. People talk to each other sometimes responding to one another with totally different conversations.

- Where you can avoid dialogue tags—he said, she demanded. Let it flow where you can, and if the dialogue is clearly from characters, then drop the speech tags.

- Create or support characterization through dialogue. Let the reader discover the character through what s/he says. Good indirect characterization keeps the reader invested and working for you in a good way.

- Show how your characters talk in dialogue. These characters drop their 'g's.' They're young and talking fast at times, so show it.

Every Given Moment
By Dan Peightel
(philosophy)

Twenty minutes ago, when I passed the Silbiger Building in Arbutus, the temperature on its digital display read 24 degrees. Christmas lights sparkled in the morning darkness. On the radio, Judy Garland sang of "olden days / Happy golden days of yore."

In half an hour, the first of my G-period students will trickle in for the semester exam. They will sharpen pencils, chatter about yesterday's biology test, ask if they can go to the bathroom. I will resist saying that I hope so.

For the moment, though, I am alone. I hear the faint hum of the room's fluorescent lights. I stare at a blinking cursor. I am more than an English teacher now. I am an adventurer, an explorer. Ironic, then, that what matters is verb tense. The present. This minute. Right now. I am at the raw edge of experience. I am alive.

On August 8, 2006, a brilliant blue Tuesday, I rose from a bench and mumbled "Whoa!" as the edges of my vision turned to green and purple fuzz. I was dead before I hit the floor. I have no memory even of falling, let alone of receiving two-rescuer CPR. People tell me that the paramedics shocked me four times before my flat-lined heart started beating again.

So, I believe in the present.

Not to the exclusion of the past or the future. Just as the most visceral verb tense, the most vital. I believe in being present. I believe in paying attention to the moment. Down the hall, a classroom door closes. I recognize the long, purposeful stride of Mr. Shearer, a talented rookie, coming toward and going past my open door. Even the most ordinary morning rushes by faster than I can comprehend. The vanilla cream doughnut I ate just before starting to write is gone, except for the sticky trace of powdered sugar left on my fingers by the cheap napkin.

To make sense of life, I must select and order what I half perceive. I must figure out what matters. Being fully present connects me to other moments, to the past and to the future. When I left my house this morning, the sparkling, windless cold intensified the roar of traffic on 95. Diesel engines growled as tractor-trailers crawled up a hill more than a mile away.

Recalling that momentary observation brings with it another morning years ago, a Sunday, just before Christmas, a *Baltimore Sun* delivery truck rumbling, late, up Wickham Road. Working to make up time, I snip bundle wires, stuff supplements in mains, load the car. Dad gets out of bed in the deep dark to drive me around my route. Later, Mom fixes Bisquick biscuits and bacon.

"The time is 7:50," Mr. Norton says over the P.A. For a moment, I can almost taste the salty sweetness of the butter on the biscuits. But the announcement continues. "Students should start making their way to their first exam."

The past lives in the present. But Dad can no longer drive, hold a conversation, or remember what happened on NCIS before the last commercial. The future is never guaranteed. The next moment is always a gift. I try to honor it by being present. I believe in paying attention.

Point: "Write a few hundred words expressing the core principles that guide your life—your personal credo." Jay Allison

Keys:
- Give a story (or maybe a couple of stories), serving as illustration of how your belief is formed or how we can see it in action.
- State your belief. Give it early and give it again near the end.
- Keep to your belief, not what you don't believe.
- Keep it as much about yourself as you can, even though you may be retelling an observation.

Music Maven: Paul McCartney's Healing Chords
By Doug Lambdin
(opinion)

Ending The Beatles' final album that they recorded together, Abbey Road, Paul McCartney trills, "And in the end, the love you take is equal to the love you make." Years later, in a mock interview given to Chris Farley on Saturday Night Live, McCartney defines that lyric in simple terms, stating, "You get what you give." To Paul McCartney, these words were not just a punchline or words on a page to fill a song; they were a real guideline for life. And, he has abided by his own message his entire career, especially when he is asked upon to give his time and music to help heal this nation.

In November of 1963, America suffered the tragedy of John F. Kennedy's assassination. There seemed to be no balm to revive the country out of its state of shock. However, on February 9, 1964, The Beatles, headed by Paul McCartney and John Lennon, arrived to perform on the Ed Sullivan Show. The jolt from the screaming fans heard by the record 73 million viewers seemed to be just the anecdote this country was yearning for to resuscitate its pulse. While the part of musical shaman was thrust upon The Beatles, Paul McCartney has comfortably assumed the role again and again.

On the clear morning of September 11, 2001, 38 years after Ed Sullivan ushered in Beatlemania, Paul McCartney and his new wife, Heather, were waiting to take off on the runway at JFK when out of their window they saw the Twin Towers fall, killing thousands before their eyes. Feeling devastated and helpless, but compelled to help anyway he could, McCartney turned to what he does best, music. Five weeks later, on October 20th, The Concert for New York, organized by McCartney, was held at Madison Square Gardens, celebrating the heroics of the police, port authority, and firefighters who served and lost their lives during the attacks. McCartney's all-star show, which included the greatest acts of the time from David Bowie to The Who, raised over 35 million to aid New Yorkers affected by the Twin Tower tragedy. And what united the crowd in the Gardens that night was Paul's song Freedom, written especially for the occasion. He went on to include the song in his encores of his upcoming record-setting world tour.

When the dust settled and America was able to return to a sense of normalcy, letting itself enjoy pastimes again, Paul McCartney would be called on yet again to patch up what had been damaged. During the 2004 Super Bowl Halftime Show performance, Janet Jackson allowed Justin Timberlake to expose her breast at the height of her final number, triggering outcries from across the nation to have some dignity, integrity, and quality entertainment restored to the family-friendly event. McCartney got the call. The following Super Bowl he wowed thousands of fans and a further billion watching on TV around the world with a string of classic Beatles hits: Get Back, Drive My Car, Hey Jude, and Wings' Live and Let Die. The next day, the critics agreed—dignity restored.

In December of 2012, to give support and aid to the victims of Hurricane Sandy, The Concert for Sandy Relief was created. Called on once again, to close the show, McCartney, headlining with other rock royalty from The Rolling Stones and The Who to Bruce Springsteen and Roger Waters, performed to lend his music and ethos to the cause. Yet, what can he still offer at 70? Sure, he brings in names. He brings in revenue. What he most keenly brings, if only for a night, is his continuity of assurance. You can 'get back to where you once belonged.' You can 'take a sad song and make it better.' Sure, it's corny. But it is what it is. That magic that only music can create. And there is no wizard more deft in his conjuring than the "cute Beatle."

Fifty years past the spark of Beatlemania, Paul McCartney is recognized as a voice of a generation and composer of the soundtrack to many of our lives. Moreover, countless bands and musicians, from Badfinger to Oasis, have given credit to the Beatles and Wings for their inspiration. His special gift of song has spanned time, cultures, and continents. Fortunately, there seems to be no bottom to McCartney's well of music and goodwill from which we draw to comfort, aid, and nurse us. And in the end, the love he makes is equal to the love he takes.

Point: Create an informed opinion piece. While it is your opinion, you can make your opinion stronger with informed support.

Keys:
- Thesis...Establish a clear assertion you're going to be supporting.
- Use anecdotal evidence. Use genuine accounts of incidences to illustrate your point. Avoid hypothetical writing.
- Transitions—bridge the differing anecdotes to give the piece cohesiveness.

Try it:
- Full-circle ending back to the beginning, to give a feeling of completeness.
- Brainstorming: What do you care about? What are you passionate about? What do you want to see changed? What wrong do you want to see made right? What do you want to see take place?

Applewood Figure
By Doug Lambdin
(art review)

His chest had sunken in to the point of being visibly concaved, like it was deflating back in on itself, as is sometimes the horrific side effect of prolonged tuberculosis (TB). But that's not why he was in the hospital; he was there for psychological treatment, the TB being a probable catalyst for his psychosis. While strolling the grounds of the Netherene Psychiatric Hospital in Surrey, England, he spied a fallen apple tree. And it was this seemingly innocuous occurrence of nature that would eventually lead to sealing his legacy, his immortality in the corner margin of the art world; for in the trunk of that tree he saw something that might speak to the world—he saw himself.

It was 1950, a time when electro-shock therapy and lobotomies were commonly prescribed for mental patients; however, Edward Adamson, a former art student and graphic designer who in WWII helped wounded patients pass hospital recovery time by creating art, had pioneered a different methodology for treating mental patients, art therapy. He gave each of his patients three things: an easel, a set of instruments, and space for self-exploration. Usually, his patients gravitated to the creative process, which could result in a simple drawing on a piece of toilet paper drawn with the charred tip of a burnt match (Although Adamson regarded every labor he received as a true work of art, he left the analysis to the physicians, feeling that the artists and doctors shouldn't be one in the same). Yet, his patient with tuberculosis had no interest in his treatment, that is, until he happened upon the fallen tree. Hospital staff then dragged the trunk in and Adamson provided the man with simple carving tools.

During the month that followed, the frail man in his early thirties, who must have nearly resembled a holocaust victim, carved, chiseled, and chipped away at the tree until it revealed a hauntingly gaunt figure that he only described as his self-portrait. The sculpted image is of a slight human with sad, listless eyes and gaping mouth and pointy, jutting hip and shoulder sockets. And most disturbingly, what the eyes are immediately drawn to is the concaved chest. One could imagine that if the wooden figure were to suddenly become incarnate, it would collapse; its body would fold in on itself, as though it could be compacted and packed away in a ventriloquist's case.

Known only as "APPLEWOOD FIGURE," the sculpture became one of the 60,000 pieces of therapy art that Adamson had amassed before his death in 1996 at the age of 84. Unfortunately, very little is known about the artist. Two years after leaving Netherene, he committed suicide. The figure he carved from a tree trunk is his only known work of art. The artist's name? Anonymous.

Donated out of Adamson's collection, which is now stored on an estate of Miriam Rothschild, APPLEWOOD FIGURE is on permanent display in the Main Building of the American Visionary Arts Museum (AVAM), situated on Key Highway at the foot of Federal Hill. The AVAM, whose "mission" is to find and display "art produced by self-taught individuals, usually without formal training, whose works arise from an innate personal vision that revels foremost in the creative act itself," is the perfect home for the figure.

Printed in big, gothic, smeared ink letters across the wall above the figure in the dimly lit gallery room is a quote by Albert Einstein: IMAGINATION IS MORE IMPORTANT THAN KNOWLEDGE. The figure stands in prominence beneath the word "IMPORTANT." And that makes me reflect on Anonymous, a moniker most often used when the artist wants to remain unknown, or disassociated with the piece, or when the artist is actually unknown. However, there is a stigma with Anonymous.

Without a name, there can't be full credit given to the artist; there's no identity. Therefore, there can't be full glory in the creation itself on behalf of the artist because no one can have a dialogue with the artist; therefore, he can't know if he has been successful or not. Thankfully, that's not why art is created. Edward Adamson stated, "Art obliges us to communicate with the inner self and, in so doing, to engage in a dialogue with our destructive and creative forces." The "anonymous" mental patient suffering from prolonged tuberculosis who created his self-portrait, APPLEWOOD FIGURE, nearly sixty years ago was in a dialogue, with himself, not us. Yet, stemming from his self-dialogue, he accomplished what all humans want—immortality. He left his mark on the world, and the world is better for it.

I have been visiting the APPLEWOOD FIGURE for the past decade. It's the first piece I visit upon entering the museum, and it's the last piece I visit before leaving. My thoughts drift back to him from time to time. For whatever reason, call it the X factor, I can't look at it enough; and each time I stand before it, I see something new, a chop mark, a smoothed chisel slash, something. And I feel closer. Understand more. I feel that there is communication. Anonymous has stretched across the ocean, across the decades, and has grabbed hold of me, just what art can do when it is at its best. So what if I don't know his name.

Adamson, Edward. Art as Healing. Coventure: London, 1984.

Point: Create a review of an art piece, or pieces.

Keys:
- Explain the work in terms of medium, genre, artist (if known), and background.
- Explain the history, how it came to be, what it was born from.
- Give an analysis of what you see as its meaning and value (not monetary).

Try it: Research the piece to give information perhaps of the artist and/or subject beyond art to add rich context.

Soundtrack
By Doug Lambdin
THE ELEVATOR (ONE-MINUTE) SPEECH

On a Monday night in 1980, December 8th to be exact, I was up well beyond my bedtime; perhaps I couldn't sleep. I was kneeling before a black and white Zenith TV, complete with tin foil rabbit ears, flipping channels, when I stopped, 18 inches from a pale, obviously shaken Howard Cosell. He was interrupting Monday Night Football coverage to report that John Lennon had just been shot and killed. I went into my bedroom, and for the first time I cried for someone other than myself. Maybe that's half true. In the year prior, I had discovered the music of The Beatles and had quickly catapulted from fan to fanatic. And like any true fan, I dreamt of a Beatles reunion, often. I had even created a 40 song set list for them to perform. But because of the actions of another fanatic, my dreams remain just that. Fast forward, I have developed a 35-year love affair with the fab four's music. I've bought the records, read the biographies, watched the movies, debated in the chat rooms, and have geeked out at the Beatle-fests. They are my soundtrack. And now, as I chauffer my kids back and forth from soccer, lacrosse, and scouts, they listen along with me to blaring CD's and remark, "Hey, these guys are pretty good."

WHAT'S LEARNED?
- I am a Beatles fan
- I am a dreamer
- I am passionate about what I like
- I have kids
- I am trying to pass on what I like
- I have felt life-changing moments deeply
- I am thoughtful about my life
- I am in my 40's now
- From lower middle-class

Task: You and another person get on an elevator at the first floor. You travel to the twentieth floor. As you go up, the other person says, "Tell me about yourself." You know you only have about a minute to give your autobiography. You can't tell him everything as there's not enough time. What do you say that gives a sense of who you are, AND what do you say that's interesting?

The Perfect PB&J: It's all in the Details
By Doug Lambdin
(process)

In kindergarten, my favorite lunch was a peanut butter and jelly sandwich. Mom served it up on my favorite Scooby Doo plate, with a tall cup of cold milk. And to this day, I still love a good PB&J. But, recreating this American delicacy is not a task to be taken lightly. It requires painstaking attention to detail. To begin, I place two fresh slices of Manischewitz seeded rye on a plate. Next, I select a wide, flat butter knife, in order to apply the peanut butter with ease. Following that, I spread the peanut butter, thickly and evenly across one slice, all the way to the edges. Afterward, I slather a dollop of Smucker's Strawberry Preserves across the opposite slice. I always put the preserves on second because it is okay to get peanut butter residue in the preserves jar, as it is refrigerated, not vice versa. Once the ingredients are in place, I add the preserves slice to the peanut butter slice, and I slice the sandwich down the middle. Slicing across corner will allow too much PB&J schmutz to ooze out. At this point, the sandwich is not ready to be eaten. I pour a tall glass of ice cold milk to drink in between bites. (As a result, my palate is cleared for the next bite.) Now, I am ready to feast. I sit in the corner of my sofa, turn on Game of Thrones, for proper ambience, and I begin to chow. While I am eating, I bite the sandwich with the preserves side up so I don't get peanut butter stuck to the roof of my mouth. Making the perfect PB&J requires loving, meticulous effort, like Mom gave. And although decades have passed since Mom made me my first PB&J, I am hooked for life.

Point: Create a how-to process, for the reader to follow, that is engaging.

Keys:
- Use non-repetitive language, especially with the transitions between steps. (Do not use first, second... or A, B...)
- Begin with a hook that grabs the reader.
- Anticipate reader questions and include reasoning for steps where needed.

Try it:
- Begin with a startling statistic, a surprising fact, or an amusing anecdote. Avoid the rhetorical question, Have you ever...
- Avoid 2nd person throughout. It's colloquial and should be used sparingly.
- For an ending go full circle back to the beginning, or make a prediction about the future. Avoid quoting someone or talking to the reader.

The Lion of Fell's Point
By Doug Lambdin
(persuasion...A letter to the Mayor of Baltimore)

Recently, I was strolling down Thames Street, looking out across the Inner Harbor, when I all but stumbled over a thigh-high, iron sculpted head. I gathered myself and studied the strong-jawed face and thick, mane-like hair, but I was at a loss. Eventually, because at my age I've read enough history and have seen enough images on the internet, I pieced together that the sculpture was of Frederick Douglass. But, that took some serious deduction. There was no name plate. No biographical plaque. Nothing. I should not have had to work that hard.

Baltimore needs to represent and celebrate this man, as well as educate present and future generations, in an artistic rendition befitting such an American Giant. Respectfully, Baltimore City must consider commissioning a monument to Frederick Douglass to be erected in the heart of Fell's Point. Frederick Douglass is one of the most significant and inspirational Americans in our history. He is the very embodiment of the American Dream and the American spirit.

As a slave living in Fell's Point, Douglass saw the value and power of education. He augmented a rudimentary education delivered upon him by a slave owner's wife, Sophia Auld, by tricking the white children in the street into spelling out the words on signs for him. He spent his saved pennies, not on food or clothes, but on

The Columbian Orator, a collection of the finest speeches to date, his fecund mind absorbing the styles and vocabulary that eventually shaped his own speeches that categorize him as one of America's finest orators, on par with Washington, Jefferson, Lincoln.

While enslaved in Fell's Point, Douglass was attacked and survived fights with other ship caulkers, holding his own, and as a result makes the decision that he will continue to assert his manhood and never back down again, even when he is sent to Mr. Covey, a "slave breaker." Covey attempted to break Douglass, and after a two-hour fist fight, Covey gave up and didn't bother Douglass again because of the threat to his reputation as a slave-breaker.

Lastly, while enslaved in Fell's Point, Douglass decided to escape to freedom because he believed that a man has the right to be free, which includes keeping the wages he has earned, as his had been taken each week by his master.

Once free, Douglass inspired other abolitionists as a writer and editor of the anti-slavery newspaper The North Star. He traveled and enthralled his audiences with his abolitionist speeches. He was integral in the creation of the black fighting regiments used for the Civil War, in which two of his sons served. He was the first black man invited to the White House, where his acquaintance with Lincoln grew. And, it is his eulogy to Lincoln delivered at the unveiling of The Freedmen's Monument that stands out as one of the most eloquent memorials to the slain president.

Frederick Douglass' influence cannot be measured; however, too many visitors, and natives, to "Charm City" have had no idea of this man's life and accomplishments while enslaved in Baltimore and after as a free man. Please support memorializing the legacy of this most important American, which will allow fellow Baltimoreans as well Charm City tourists to be enlightened and inspired.

Point: Write to persuade to have your audience act upon something or alter a belief/perspective.

Keys:
- Explain what you want to take place.
- Explain the need for it.
- Explain the value, for whom it is valuable, and how it is valuable.
- Always give evidence to bolster your assertions.

Try it: Consider your tone. Be assertive, even giving a sense of urgency, but not combative nor full of contempt.

300 Word Sentence
By Doug Lambdin

Thinking that pit bull dogs, American Staffordshire Terriers, an American breed of strong, muscular terriers, originally developed in England, with a short, close-lying, stiff coat of any color or combination of colors except solid white, are dogs that are ferocious, aggressive, and dangerous to children and the elderly, and believing that a pit bull's nature is to attack anything and anyone without provocation because he had read so many of the stories in the media that maligned and stereotyped pit bulls, my father, an overly cautious man, who became weary of aggressive dogs while he was a door-to door salesman, a job that brought him into daily contact with different breeds of dogs that seemed to be waiting to prey on unsuspecting intruders, barking and nipping at salesman's ankles as they walk up the sidewalks towards the front door in order to try to sell his latest product from Kimball Piano and Organ Music Company, a company that sells pianos and organs through the use of in-home instrument trials, searched the Internet, looking for a docile and trusting breed of dog to buy as an early Christmas present for me and my sister, both of us serious dog-lovers, who had been hounding our father to buy a dog for us for Christmas, for years; however, as my father searched the Internet, which became a long and arduous labor of love to please his two kids, the prides and joys of his life, finding multiple dog-friendly sites that discussed in chat-boards and in professionally written articles about the temperaments of dogs, rating them from best to worst dog to be around children, he began to discover that pit bulls have always been one of the most trusted canine breeds to be around children and the elderly, being noted for their loyalty and eagerness to please, not for any propensity to be harmful, which, it turns out, is a false representation of these playful, loving best friends to man.

Word Count: 328

Point: The 300-word sentence is an exercise in sentence control and using modifiers.

Keys:
- Use all the modifiers at your disposal, but avoid using the same one over and over. Remember, bad repetition resonates as much as good repetition.
- Only use one semicolon. That means that there are only two independent clauses here. (See the underlined above.)
- Wherever there is a noun that needs an explanation or be put into context, use a modifier.

Don't try it:
No lists. That's cheating.
No parenthesis.
No multiple adjectives beyond three.

Taxiing in the UK
By Doug Lambdin
Published in *BootsnAll* and *Travellers' Impressions*
(travel)

I know that the first thing anyone should tell you to do when you visit any city is to get out and walk the streets and avenues to get a genuine feel for what the city has to offer, right? But I'm not going to say that. Instead, I say don't get out, make sure you get in – a taxi that is. For a true visceral experience and to truly enjoy a London institution, make an effort to take a load off those tired, tourist-worn feet and experience taxiing the way it should be done, by professionals.

Now if you're from the States as I am, the thought of taking a taxicab sends your pulse racing about as much as a trip to the supermarket. But that's because a ride in a cab for us is being cramped sideways in back of smelly car while being ignored by the driver who is on the cell-phone to his girlfriend (this part I imagine because I can't understand what language he speaks) and worrying how far out of the way we're being routed to run up the meter. Let's face it, Jerry Seinfeld was right: The only qualification you need to be a cab driver in the States is to just have a face. This is why I was so taken aback by the experience my wife and I had this summer while traveling through the UK.

Exiting Heathrow Airport, the driver gave us a friendly smile as greeted us with an "Allo" and opened the black door for us to step into the back of his regally spacious taxi, offering more legroom than the passenger side of my own sedan. We stretched out in the back seat and I couldn't help thinking that if this car was available for hire when I went to my senior prom, I would gladly have shelled out the bucks.

As soon as we were free of the congestion of Heathrow's traffic, our driver, Terry, as we soon found out, engaged us in conversation. By the time we reached our B&B, we were old friends. He told us that we must try Yorkshire pudding but keep away from any Shepherd's Pie that wasn't homemade, like his wife's. (We were half expecting an invitation.) At the hotel, Terry, not walked, but ran our luggage up to the front door. I wouldn't have been surprised at all if he would have checked us in and carried our bags straight up to our room. After we over-tipped him, he tipped his cap and wished us well. I miss Terry.

Thinking that drivers like Terry were a fluke couldn't be further from the truth. Each excursion proved to be more enchanting than the last. We became acquainted with as many friendly people and learned as much about the history of the city as any other tourist who paid hundreds of dollars more to an agent to travel with a guided group. What was nicer was that the tour guides guided us alone.

One evening, coming back from Soho, we stepped into the taxi at front of the line. (That's how it's done: Taxis line up along the curb and whoever is at the head of the line, he gets the fare, keeping the competition fair.) Recognizing that we weren't locals, our driver asked if we were enjoying our trip and asked what we had visited so far. After we listed the usual London must-sees, Buckingham Palace, Trafalgar Square, Tower of London, etc., he said he'd point out some landmarks to us to add to our list. He pointed out Hyde Park and a couple of other parks and then proceeded to give us the background on one of his "favorites:" The Admiralty Arch. We turned onto a crescent avenue, and he pointed.

"That's the arch there...Used to house the 'sea lords.' Cost over a million pounds sterling."

Once again, we freely over-tipped.

On a separate afternoon, we went on a hunt for catalogs from some local magic shops to give to my dad, who dabbles in conjuring. When I asked the driver, Wallace, to take me to a shop I had found in the phone book, he asked me if I was in the "Brotherhood of Magicians? I know where they meet every week." After I told him my reason, he answered, "Oh no, Davenport's is where you want to go. If your dad knows anything about magic, he'd have heard of Davenport's." Dad was quite jealous that I had been to Davenport's. And I was jealous of London for having Wallace.

This treatment was the same all over the UK: Bath, The Cotswolds, Edinburgh, and everywhere else we went. Why? Maybe it is the culture. And maybe, as we learned, it is because the drivers are proud professionals who study and train for up to two years to drive these taxicabs, not as a job in between jobs, but as a career.

If you travel to London, there is definitely one thing that you must do. Tour the Tower of London? Certainly.

See Buckingham Palace? Of course. Let yourself be covered with pigeons in Trafalgar Square? That goes without saying. (Mind the poo.) But above all, ride the taxis – a tip rarely found in the travel brochures. And if you see Terry or Wallace, tell them I said, "Allo."

Point: This is a travel piece. Your reader wants to experience this place you are writing about. This goes beyond beautiful photographs. This is a story, but a story full of details and flavors of the place, making the reader want to go and share in that experience.

Keys:
- Tell your story. Find that moment that elevated your experience and tell it.
- Remember, you are not writing about a whole trip here, just one aspect of it. The focus is on taking taxis. Then the focus is narrowed to two great experiences while taking a taxi.
- Slow down and put us there. You cannot use a descriptive word like "amazing," if we cannot see what was amazing.
- Do not go off on a tangent because you have to tell us about something else. It won't fit.

Try It:
- If people are represented, try some dialogue, but only what's needed, a highlight of what was spoken.

No Way Out
By Dan Peightel
(two-person realistic scene)

Length: variable (takes place at one time, in one place; change of time or place = new scene)

Task: Put two characters with opposing desires in some place where they are forced to confront their differences, and let us see and hear their actions and reactions as each of them attempts to get what he or she wants, or attempts to block the other's desires.

Keys to Success:
- Have something important at stake. Fiction and drama present heightened reality. Not every conflict must be life or death, but it must force the characters to act. Raise the stakes on real life. For example, instead of you just getting detention in sixth grade, have your eighth-grade character refuse to sit down when Sr. Mary Mark tells him to be quiet.
- Have a beginning, middle, and end. Good scenes (like good stories) start with a situation that gets disrupted. Something goes wrong. That causes a chain of action and reaction. Things get worse. Until one character prevails (at least momentarily), resulting in a new situation. Within that familiar structure, show action that is both inevitable and surprising.

- Tell lies to reveal the truth. For example, if your pet canary died, write a first-person story about the death of a grade school friend (who's actually alive and well, but who goes to another high school). You remember the feelings of loss when the canary died and when your friend changed schools, and you write a story about losing a person forever.

- Be interesting. Keep readers reading. And be convincing. It's hard to tell a good lie. Every detail has to be authentic. And has to fit naturally with everything else. If there's one loose thread, people will find it. Even if the events in your scene are entirely made up, your readers should believe that those events actually happened.

Models:

"Flight Risk" (novel excerpt)
"Flight Risk" (screenplay excerpt)

Potential Uses:
- As a stand-alone short story or short film
- As part of a longer story or full-length script
- As a technique for finding and bringing to life key moments of a memoir (with the restriction that the characters, events, and dialogue must be as true as memory and evidence will allow)

Read as a Writer:
- What are the strengths of the narrative version of the scene from *Flight Risk*?
- What are its weaknesses or limitations?
- What are the strengths of the dramatic version of the scene from *Flight Risk*?
- What are its weaknesses or limitations?
- What similarities exist between the two versions?
- What can one do that the other cannot?

Try one of these scenarios:
- A teenager is stuck in a car with a prying parent during a traffic jam on the way home after a bad day of school. The parent wants to know. The kid doesn't want to tell. Is it the mother or the father? How are those two stories different?
- Your eighth grader has just been accepted to MSJ, but when Sister Mary Mark keeps him after school, he refuses to apologize because he thinks she's being unfair. What does she think? How far will each of them go?
- For now, you MAY NOT write scenes about commando teams or DEA agents or galactic warriors. If you really want to write about war, try one of these scenarios:
  1. A week before starting high school, a fourteen-year-old boy learns that his father is being deployed to Afghanistan (or that his father's deployment has been extended). Who tells him the news? Where? How does he react?

2. A boy proclaims his anti-war stance at school and has to defend himself against a kid who calls him unpatriotic. What if that kid is the boy whose father's deployment was extended? What if he punches the anti-war kid?

Flight Risk
By Dan Peightel
(novel excerpt)

Brian Russell hung up his office phone. Lund wanted to see him. Right away. Russell rubbed his temples and stared out the window at the con trail of a jet streaking across a perfect blue sky. He imagined himself on a beach sipping a drink with a little paper umbrella. He got up from his high-back leather chair, unrolled his shirt sleeves, and buttoned his cuffs. Any beach would do, as long as nobody from MTI's Wasatch Division could reach him, as long as he didn't have to make ten decisions an hour about costs versus safety.

Russell turned his head slowly left and then back right to relieve the tension in his neck. Just as he exhaled, Roger Boisjoly appeared in Russell's office doorway. Instantly, Russell's shoulders tightened, and the tension was worse.

Boisjoly reminded Russell of a younger version of himself, right down to the short-sleeve shirt, the pocket protector, and the too-wide tie. The younger man was a top-notch engineer, but he had the social skills of a robot. Russell knew that Boisjoly was back to pester him again about the damned o-rings.

"Brian," Boisjoly said, "When is Lund going to quit dragging his feet on the o-ring team?"

"There's not going to be an o-ring team."

"What?"

"NASA's comfortable with the risk."

"Comfortable with the risk?" Boisjoly said. "What the hell does that mean?"

"Jim Thomas, over at Marshall…"

"Jesus, Brian," Boisjoly said. "What did you tell him? Does he even know…"

"I told him just what you told me."

Boisjoly pivoted, as if he might walk out. But he spun all the way around and stepped toward Russell. Without a word, the younger man reddened and thrust his chin and chest forward like he expected to go at it with some drunk in a bar. Russell stepped back reflexively.

"You need to settle down," Russell said.

"Settle down?" Boisjoly said. "We're talking about lives here, Brian."

Russell slid past Boisjoly and closed the office door. No need for the whole damned department to hear. Enough of the others already resented Boisjoly's blunt, confrontational style. They complained that he was just too hard to work with.

"We're always talking about lives," Russell said. "A certain amount of risk…"

"You need to make them understand," Boisjoly said. "If they don't care about the orbiter, tell them they damn well might lose the launch pad, too."

Russell's jaw clenched. "You don't get it, Roger." He forced himself to stop, to breathe, to keep from shouting. He spoke each word of his next sentence distinctly. "They do understand."

"Then let me tell them," Boisjoly said. "I'll…"

"You'll what, Roger?" Russell removed his suit

jacket from a hanger on the back of the office door.

"What do you want me to do? Write a damn suicide note?"

"If that's what it takes." The words hung in the air for a second. Even Boisjoly seemed to recognize what he was asking. But then he just kept going. "If we're both agreed..."

Russell cut him off. "It doesn't make a damn bit of difference. It's NASA's call." Boisjoly paced back and forth like a caged lion. It was all so simple for him. But Russell thought about all the jobs at Wasatch. He thought about his daughter at Vanderbilt, about the mortgage on his house. It wasn't just this contract, but the next one, and the one after that. That's why Lund was so angry about Boisjoly's memo. Russell shrugged into his suit jacket. "Our job," he said, "is to present them with the information."

Boisjoly stopped suddenly, right in front of Russell. "Screw the protocol, Brian. Stick your neck out. For once in your life..."

"I am sticking my neck out."

"By letting them think what they want?"

Sidestepping Boisjoly, Russell buttoned his shirt collar, cinched his tie, and moved toward the door. He yanked it open. The meeting was over. But Boisjoly lingered, waiting for an answer. So Russell gave him one, loud enough for the others to hear.

"I'm on my way upstairs," he said. "To try to save your job." Boisjoly looked genuinely baffled. And, for a moment, Russell enjoyed that. "Lund thinks you're a loose cannon. I've got to go tell him what a brilliant engineer you are."

Flight Risk
By Dan Peightel
(screenplay excerpt)

INT. – Offices of MTI Wasatch Division   DAY

BRIAN RUSSELL, 45, hangs up his phone, rubs his temples, gets up from his high-back leather chair, unrolls his shirt sleeves and buttons his cuffs.

Just then, ROGER BOISJOLY, 30, in short sleeves and a too-wide tie, appears in Russell's office doorway

                    BOISJOLY
          Brian, when is Lund going to quit
          dragging his feet on the o-ring team?

                    RUSSELL
          There's not going to be an o-ring team.

                    BOISJOLY
          What are you talking about?

                    RUSSELL
          NASA's comfortable with the risk.

                    BOISJOLY
          Comfortable with the risk? What the
          hell does that mean?

RUSSELL
Jim Thomas, over at Marshall—

BOISJOLY
(interrupting)
Jesus, Brian, what did you tell him?
Does he even know—

RUSSELL
(overlapping)
I told him just what you told me.

BOISJOLY pivots as if he might walk out, but spins all the way around and comes a step closer. He's ready to go toe-to-toe.

RUSSELL
(continuing)
You need to settle down.

BOISJOLY
Settle down?!

RUSSELL slides past him.

In the outer office, TWO SECRETARIES and a MAN WITH THICK GLASSES turn their heads toward the raised voices.

RUSSELL closes the office door.

BOISJOLY
(continuing)
We're talking about lives here, Brian.

RUSSELL
We're always talking about lives. A
certain amount of risk—

BOISJOLY
(interrupting)
You need to make them understand. If
they don't care about the orbiter, tell
them they damn well might lose the
launch pad, too.

RUSSELL
(straining to stay calm)
You don't get it, Roger. They do
understand.

BOISJOLY
Then let me tell them. I'll—

RUSSELL
You'll what, Roger? What do you want
me to do? Write a damn suicide note?

BOISJOLY
If that's what it takes. If we're both

agreed—

                    RUSSELL
                (interrupting)
            It doesn't make a damn bit of
            difference. It's NASA's call.

BOISJOLY paces back and forth, like a caged lion.

                    RUSSELL
                (continuing)
            It's our job to present them with the
            information.

BOISJOLY stops suddenly right in front of RUSSELL.

                    BOISJOLY
            Screw the protocol, Brian. Stick your
            neck out. For once in your life—

                    RUSSELL
                (interrupting)
            I am sticking my neck out.

                    BOISJOLY
            Letting them think what they want to
            think?

RUSSELL shrugs into his suit jacket and moves toward the
door. He opens it. The meeting's over. BOISJOLY lingers,

waiting for an answer.

                    RUSSELL
          I'm on my way upstairs to try to save
          your job. Lund thinks you're a loose
          cannon. I've got to go tell him what a
          brilliant engineer you are.

Images and Lines – (short free verse poem)

Length: 10 – 50 lines

Task:
Without using rhyme or a fixed rhythm, write a poem about a person, an object, or an experience that you encounter every day.

Keys to Success:
- Listen for a line, a bit of sound. Follow it. What do you taste? Scribble more lines in your journal. Which ones seem to connect? Search for images that evoke emotion. Smell the oiled leather of your first baseball glove, and let it lead you to the sadness you felt pushing your bike up Williston Street, toward home and a summer sunset.

- Break sentences / into lines. Sometimes broken / sentences have more meanings / than whole sentences. / Pull readers on / to the next line with the same / word that makes them pause / to think about the current line. / Poetry often takes wild, / dangerous leaps. The best poetry / leaves a swinging trapeze / for the reader to grab.

- Raise the intensity of ordinary language. For example, pay attention to the beginning sounds of words. Listen for lines that linger in the air, that remain in the mind, because the consonants build power. Use the principle of repetition and variation. Set up a pattern. Then, just when readers expect it, break or bend or twist it.

Models:
"Innings"
"Squeaks"
"Tips for New Poets"
"Love Left Unspoken"
"The Heirloom in My Garden"

Note: Some poetry rhymes. But most doesn't. A fixed rhythm can give a poem power. But not if it clip-clops along mechanically. For now, learn to do other things with sound.

Potential Uses:
- As a stand-alone poem publishable in *The Carpenter*
- As part of a thematic collection that you compile and publish as a booklet
- As a printed piece to accompany a photograph in an album or exhibition
- As a gift for a relative or friend, perhaps someone who shared the experience with you
- As something you pair with a drawing and read to children, just for the delight of sound

Read as a Writer:
How does "Innings" make use of repetition? Of variation? How does "Squeaks" avoid becoming a rhyming poem?

Why does it do so?

How does "Tips for New Poets" alter the conventions of a typical set of instructions?

How does "Heirloom..." make use of narrative?

Try:

- including a wish or a lie in every line
- mentioning a different place in every line
- making a strange comparison in every line
- building each new stanza (group of lines) around a different one of your five senses
- alternating the beginning of every other line between "I used to be ... / But now I am ..." changing the pattern in the next stanza to "Now that I ... / I wish people would ..."

Innings
By Dan Peightel

The first opens
awaiting the ghost
on the ramparts of Elsinore.

The second settles
back, a Sunday driver
touring the park.

The third wanes, the old moon
heralding the return
of the leadoff hitter.

The fourth crawls,
the clock at two when
quitting time is five.

The fifth gambles,
sticks with the hand
the house has dealt.

The sixth ends the beginning
and begins the end, turns the
sonnet from was to will be.

The seventh leans forward, glances east
at empty highway, west at the setting sun,
stretches, yawns, and resumes its rocking.

The eighth wonders and worries
a week before payday, budgets
or borrows just to stay even.

The ninth preaches salvation
on every pitch, asks if you still
believe in the promise of redemption.

Squeaks
By Dan Peightel

Squeaks sneak nearly unnoticed from
the endless zigs and zags of basketball,
leak from rubber soles on wet tile floors.
Each unique squeak barely, bravely,
ekes out its own brief (bleak?) existence.
Meek squeaks come from mice
and the beaks of baby birds.
Desks squeak in a boring class where
no one ever speaks without permission.
Squeaks creak out of bolts, wallets, and minds—
anything turned, squeezed, or closed too tight.
Squeaks shriek out of rusty bicycle chains
and the freaky doors of antique mansions.
Squeaks play peek-a-boo,
pique the curiosity of children, librarians, and mechanics,
tweak the ears of those who would catch them in the act.

Tips for New Poets
By Dan Peightel

Don't be intimidated
by the word
poem,
by the imposing idea,
the impending doom.

You're just writing
sentences
and breaking them
into lines.

You can capitalize
beginnings of lines—
or not. But sprinkle
commas only
where they belong,
not at the end
of every line.

Talk about love
without talking
about love, but
by showing us
a busted knuckle
on a father's greasy
hand, chapped raw
from the cold, and

tightening another
bolt on another Benz
that'll never be his.

Fly to the moon
on paper wings
and dream dreams
of ancient castles,
truthful lies, and
orange apples.

Love Left Unspoken
By Dan Peightel

Side lit, immersed in shadow,
her face entices darkness—
this woman, Frances, who
could have been my mother,
whom my father wanted to love,
would have loved, if she'd ever
noticed he was there alone.

It's perhaps his best picture,
even my mother says so.
I wonder if she knows,
if he ever told her,
what taking it must have meant
to a seventeen-year-old boy
who needed his camera to talk.

In other pictures Frances is only
a girl, silly bangs and teeth too large.
Here, though, chin resting on bare knee,
pouting, she knows how to whisper.

He wasn't like George Rock
and those other City College boys.
Busy with composing, with checking
shutter speed and aperture and focus,
he would joke and make her giggling
friends forget and be themselves.

Posing for it was surely her idea.
Gazing at her image reversed on the
ground-glass screen, at the very image
of love, at a moment he couldn't hold,
he spoke only once, softly,
to coax her to tilt her chin.

My father never knew
how to talk about feelings.
But once, when I was in college
and Julie's kind rejection was more
than I thought I could bear,
he told me about the woman
in the picture. It was on the way
to pick up Mom at the beauty shop.
"Instead, I married your mother.
Then we had you guys and all."

The Heirloom in My Garden
By Doug Lambdin
Published in *Chattels of the Heart*
and in *The Journal of Pastoral Care and Counseling*

Who was it who said
that we are an accident, that existence
is a fluke, that there is no God?

Whoever it was,
he must not have a garden.
But I do.

I have a vegetable garden.
On light August evenings,
in the dropping humid heat,

I kneel in my patch
and pick ripe tomatoes
for the evening's supper.

Before my bowl is full,
I can stand it no longer.
I pluck a small red and yellow heirloom

and hold it to my nose,
breathing in sweetness and earth,
feeling the smooth, natural coolness.

I sink my teeth in and draw

my mouth closed, quickly slurping
as much of the juice as possible

as the excess, rushing down my wrist
and forearm, stops and spreads
in the hem of my short sleeve.

The small fruit is candy,
sweet and tender. A gift,
heavy and taut with sun and water.

Before I finish one, I know
I will have another.
And so, I sit back on my heels.

This can't be an accident, I think.
This can't be a fluke.
There must be a God.

18 Staples
By Doug Lambdin
Published in the anthology *Listening to the Birth of Crystals*
(short free verse)

18 staples
Down my father's chest.
Do they bother you? I ask.
I don't know, he replies.
I haven't looked yet.

I Awake at Three
By Dan Peightel
(a villanelle)

I awake at three, terrified of a future all alone.
My muse sleeps undisturbed in the smothering dark.
Rising, I shower and dress, as if the day were my own.

A voice from childhood calls me repeatedly to the phone,
Where some fond hope is skewered on an overheard
remark. I awake at three, terrified of a future all alone.

Just a day ago, I spent hours dulled by the drone
Of a system designed to snuff all creative spark.
Rising, I shower and dress, as if today might be my own.

Aboard a lover's cruise, all I want is an ice cream cone,
But the faceless purser insists it's time to disembark.
I awake at three, terrified of a future all alone.

Restless now, and tossing, I find no hint of the proper tone
For discussing the mysteries of creation or the quark.
Rising, I shower and dress, as if I would make today my own.

The porches all are swept, the lawns all are mown.
At the edge of a silken dream, I hear a warning bark.
I awake at three, terrified of a future all alone.
Rising, I shower and dress, as if my little life were my own.

Point: Create a villanelle poem—a 19-line poem, containing an ABA rhyme pattern throughout. The 1st line is repeated in the 6th, 12th, and 18th lines. And, the 3rd line is repeated in the 9th, 15th, and 19 lines.

The effect: Those repeating lines that leap frog each other will finally marry at the end, creating a momentum for their being connected.

Keys:
- Create the first stanza. Before you continue, create a rhyme arsenal for your a and B rhymes. If your 2nd line ends with the word "orange," you'll find it too hard to continue.
- Create a narrative that moves across lines and maybe even stanzas. 19 lines doesn't mean 19 sentences.
- Put time into creating those repetitive lines because they will have the great effect.

Little Gunpowder
By Doug Lambdin
(a sestina)

When I was a boy, my father would take me to the Little
                                                    Gunpowder
to skip
stones.
We'd stand at the creek's edge
and skim rocks
across the water's surface.

The surface
of the Little Gunpowder
cushioned, cradled, and catapulted the rocks
until the zing and propulsion of the skips
eased to the point that the edges
of each stone,

and then the entire stone,
slipped beneath the surface.
One time at the edge
of the Little Gunpowder,
my breath skipped
and I dropped my rock

as my father's rock
echoed, Dad's gonna be living somewhere else from now
                                                    on. The stone
at my feet, unskipped,

lay there on the bank's surface,
the Little Gunpowder
spreading out and away before us, beyond the edge

of the reeds and the edge
of the big rocks
where it seemed that the Little Gunpowder
dropped off the earth. I'll never skip a stone
that far across the surface.
That would take a hundred skips!

We skipped
the rest of the stones piled in a heap at the edge.
On the surface,
steady, two rocks,
our faces, two stones,
at our feet, the Little Gunpowder.

Deep beneath the surface of the Little Gunpowder,
far from the edge, lay all those rocks
still, stone after stone, forever skipped.

Selfie Sestina
by Doug Lambdin

And this one's me,
standing on the edge.
I almost dropped my selfie
stick, reaching out to fit in my whole face,
trying not to fall
before I post.

Everybody loves my posts.
They love me!
They're gonna absolutely fall
in love with how close I am to the edge.
Should I do duck face?
Hmmm. Not my best selfie.

My best selfie
is posting
with kissie face.
Me
alone in the pic from edge to edge.
Who couldn't fall

for that? I don't want to fall
back on my usual selfie,
just standing on the edge
scrolling through a hundred pics to post
of me
giving backwards peace sign by my face.

I know! The surprised I'm-having-the-most-amazing-time-
ever-face!
I'll act like I'm falling.
"Watch me!"
All by myself
about to post
from the edge of the edge.

I think I need to get even closer to the edge
for my face's
post
to fall
into place and for myself
to be happy with me.

Aaaaahhhhhh! The edge is falling
away from me and my face. Wait! Best! Selfie!
Ever! Click. Post. Look at me! Look at me!

Point: A sestina has the boundary of end-word repetition. Forcing your narrative to keep going back to these words is often where the poetry occurs. Those words take on more meanings. Very often the effect is that you create something more interesting than you would have expected.

Keys:
- When beginning, just create a few lines without worrying about end-word choice. Then, look at your lines and decide which words you think you could keep coming back to. Also, you can use different forms of the word: hope, hopefully, hopelessness, etc.
- The concluding stanza, or the envoi, does have a specific sequence of end-word usage, but most folks bend that rule. As long as you have two words per line and one of them ends the line, that will work.
- Tell a story, instead of making 39 observational statements about something.
- Avoid repeating your message.

Try it:
- Just because a line ends does not mean that the sentence needs to end. A sestina has 39 lines, but this one has only nine sentences. And, a sentence can spread across stanzas.
- Try www.dilute.net/sestinas for an automatic template to use for your sestina.

GIN!
By Doug Lambdin
Published in *Modern Haiku*

GIN!
His catheter drips

deep
deep
gold

3 finches
By Doug Lambdin
Published in *SNAPSHOTS*

3 finches on the wire
my father strums Gershwin
on the marble stoop

rearview mirror
By Doug Lambdin
Published in *SNAPSHOTS*

rearview mirror
my father's forehead
replacing mine

Point: Create a brief, observational haiku poem.

Keys:
- Economy, economy, economy. A haiku should be as brief as possible. Shed words you do not need at all, like articles and linking verbs. Perhaps think of 5/7/5 as the maximum.
- Also, a haiku usually juxtaposes two things in a single observation. Observe and record two images in the real world that can be seen/felt in relation to another. What the casual observer gloss over and miss? This is not forcing a moment into poetry, but it is recording the poetry of a moment, as one would through the lenses of a camera.
- Avoid abstractions (ideas) or non-concrete images. For example, "beautiful." Beauty is an idea. Plus, if you have to say "beautiful," then you haven't done your job with the image. If it is not discernible with any of the five senses, do not record it.

Note: The above examples are western haiku, not Japanese.

When Japanese translates into English, there are usually three lines totaling 17 syllables, or 5/7/5. There is always a word indicating the season, for example "blossom;" you would not write "Spring." And, both images occur in nature. It is a single moment. So, you would not write, "snow filling the woods." That is a movie, not a snapshot.

Professional Email
By Erin Van Bavel

Guidelines:
Include a brief but informative subject.
Follow letter format.

Use proper grammar and spelling. Proofread and double-check your email before you send. It might help to read your email aloud to make sure have captured the appropriate tone.

Know your purpose. Do not ramble. Be concise.

Keep introductions brief. Remember that you can include contact information under your signature.

If you have a reason to express gratitude, do it first so that it does not seem like an afterthought.

Follow a standard structure:
- greeting/salutation
- a compliment or pleasantry
- expression of thanks
- the reason for your email (Why are you emailing them)
- a call to action (What is the action that you need them to do?)
- a closing message
- signature

Example:
(SUBJECT: Solutions Showcase Interview)

Dear Coach Smith,
I hope you are well. Thank you so much for all the pointers you gave me after practice last week. I really appreciate your help.

Could I interview you for my Solutions Showcase project? I am creating a documentary that explains the relationship between team sports and overall academic achievement. I would like to hear your opinion and discuss my ideas with you. Please let me know when I can stop by your classroom to interview you.

I appreciate your consideration and hope that we can meet soon. Your expertise will help me improve my project. I look forward to talking with you soon.

Sincerely,

Joe Gael
jgael@msjnet.net
Homeroom 415

Handwritten Thank-You Note
By Erin Van Bavel

(Address to be written on envelope):

Mr. Joe Gael
123 Purple Lane
Baltimore, MD 21228

(Handwritten thank-you note format):

May 4, 2018

Dear _____,

Thank you so much for helping to judge our Solutions Showcase presentations on Wednesday. Your feedback was really helpful for our growth as writers, thinkers, and creators.

Sincerely,

Solutions Showcase Progress Report (A)
By Erin Van Bavel

Name
Section
Teacher
Date

Solutions Showcase Progress Report

Project Summary:

What is your project? Why are you doing it? Briefly describe in complete sentences.

Essential Question:

Type the essential question that you will answer with your project.

Progress:

To date, I have accomplished the following: write a paragraph in complete sentences that describes the work that has been done. You may use bullet points to clarify but the bulk of this sentence will be written in paragraph form.

Additional Work:

By DATE, I will accomplish to following: write a paragraph in complete sentences that specifically describes your next steps. Include the deadline.

Remaining Questions:

The following questions remain. They are essential to my project because.... I will need to do the following steps in order to answer these questions. Use complete sentences. You may use bullet points to clarify.

Expected Results:

This is the overall expected result(s) for my project. I expect to present my results to _____ on DATE _____.

Solutions Showcase Progress Report (B)
By Erin Van Bavel

Project Summary:

I plan to create a driveway workout system. I am doing this because my family members enjoy playing sports and we need a way to practice our skills at home. I will focus on drills and exercise that will improve our overall fitness and our skills as athletes. A driveway workout system is less expensive and more convenient than a gym membership.

Essential Question:

Can I create an affordable, semi-permanent system that incorporates elements of cardiovascular and technical skills training?

Progress:

To date, I have researched DIY sites on the Internet to gather ideas for my own driveway workout system.

Additional Work:

- By March 3, I will create a blueprint of my design.
- By March 4, I will write an informative report that details the types of exercise and technical skills that I want
- to include in my system.

- By March 5, I will email my son's coaches and my neighbor, a high school athlete, to gain their perspective on what skills are necessary to practice. I will use their feedback to improve my design.
- By March 6, I will have an updated design and will begin looking for materials. I hope to stick to a budget of $100.
- By the end of March, I will finish my Power Point presentation.

Remaining Questions:

- How can I create a system that meets the needs of my entire family (adults and kids, ages 9, 7 and 5) How can I make my system durable enough that my kids won't destroy it?
- How can I get the word out to other parents who want to build a driveway system?
- How will I present my "story" to the judges? How will I publish my work?

Schedule for workouts

Expected Results:

This is the overall expected result(s) for my project. I expect to present my results to my students on April 9, 2018.

Proposal
By Dan Peightel

Joe Schmoe
ENGL 210 – Period Z
December 6, 2018

Split Second: Images of Athletes in Action

I love sports. But, at best, I am an average athlete. The only way I'm going to make it to the pros is with my camera—a Nikon D40X. So, I want to use Solutions Showcase as an opportunity to improve my chances of someday working as a photographer for *Sports Illustrated*.

From my current experience with photography, I have many questions—about technical skills, about equipment, about planning and preparation, and about making contacts. But my essential question is this: How can I begin, right now, to build my career as a sports photographer?

The simple answer, it seems to me, is to produce publishable – or, better yet, published – sports photographs. I may not be able to control whether my pictures get published. But I can control how many shots I take, edit, and send out. To give myself the best chance of having my photographs published, I will challenge myself to meet the following targets:

- photograph at least three sporting events per week between now and May 1st
- shoot at least 250 frames at each event
- select and edit at least ten images from each event
- send out at least 15 images each week to *The Quill*, *The Tower*, local sports publications (such as *The Catonsville Times*), and online outlets (such as the MIAA website).

To improve my chances of getting great shots, I will also take the following steps:

- talk to Mr. Loovis (athletic director) about getting sideline access at MSJ home games
- read books and online guides about the techniques of action photography
- talk to Mr. Foti, who teaches photography at MSJ, about tips and techniques
- study photographs in current issues of *Sports Illustrated* and *ESPN Magazine*
- study the work of Neil Leifer and Charles M. Conlon, photographers who produced famous sports photographs in the days before the Zoom lens and the auto-drive.
- look for a professional sports photographer who might serve as my mentor
- contact the Ravens about how to apply for sideline credentials (you never know!)

For my presentation to the judges in May, I will create a web-based photographic portfolio documenting the winter and spring sports seasons at MSJ. This will have real value for *The Quill* and *The Tower*. By Tuesday, December 11, I will talk with Mr. Schultheis (*Quill*) and Mr. Hughes (*Tower*) to learn what assignments, requirements, and deadlines they might have.

Sample Progress Report from Mr. Peightel

The title of my project is "The Man from Yesterday."

The question I need to answer is this:

What experiences from my past have most shaped who I am today?

I am creating a collection of personal essays entitled "Music out of Baltimore," to help me better understand myself. And to help me better explain myself to the world, especially to my students, friends, and family.

The three most impressive things I have to show are

1. An essay entitled "The Price of Respect," about Br. Brian Vetter, my teacher for Honors Freshman English. This essay makes use of a number of reversals. First, there is the difference between who I thought Brother Brian was when I was a student and who he turned out to be when I knew him as a colleague. Then there is the difference between Brother's life here at the Mount and the service he was called to in Bolivia. And, finally, there is the difference between who I was at fourteen and who I have become as a teacher. All of that leads me to consider whether or not I can live up to the model provided by Brother Brian. I can only hope that I have what it takes to pay the price of respect.

2. An essay entitled "Music out of Baltimore," about how the events of one Friday night in 1971 reflect the tensions my parents faced in trying to provide a good life for my brother and me. The thing I love best about this essay is its use of detail and dialogue to imply tension. For example, when my mother gives in to my brother and me about going out for a late-night Harley Burger, readers know that her answer is really directed at our father. Her worries about whether they can afford to splurge on hamburgers are really about how they will pay for tuition and whether they can buy a bigger house in the county. This one incident suggests the history of tones in my parents' marriage.

3. An essay entitled "At the Hour of Our Death," about my relationship with Br. James Kelly and what his life and death taught me about trying to live my own life. I am especially proud of how the essay uses emails from Brother James to capture his voice and set up the pep talk I "imagine" him giving, "phrased in the imperative," in the final two lines. When people first read the essay, they seem to feel that Brother actually speaks those final lines. Upon re-reading, of course, they realize that those lines are the narrator's interpretation of what Brother implied when he talked about facing one's own mortality.

I also have several other essays, written over many years, that I may include in my final collection. These include:

- "The Pose That Love Remembers," about a photograph that my father took of my mother just after they were engaged

- "Learning to See," about a photograph that my father took at the Inner Harbor's Pier 5 (in front of the Baltimore Gas & Electric power plant) when he was seventeen, and that hung in our basement and captured my imagination when I was a kid

- "My Father's People," about my father's parents and siblings before, during, and after a photograph he took of them unpacking a picnic lunch at a rest stop on a trip to Hagerstown

- "Dreams and Obligations," about a photograph that my father took of me scoring the winning run in a Little League baseball game

- "Where I Was When Elvis Died," about the summer of 1977, when my first girlfriend broke up with me

- "On Small Talk and Living," about an encounter that I had with another photographer while I was shooting pictures of surfers in Ocean City, and about what the encounter reveals about the similarities and differences between my father and me.

The most difficult thing about producing these results was

the amount of time and effort required to produce a finished essay. My most recent essay, "A Song or Two," explores contradictions between belief and action by weaving together stories about music, sports, history, politics, and family. After more than three months of exploration, research, thinking, and note-taking between early-August and mid-November 2016, writing the essay required 43 drafting sessions between November 11, 2016 and February 1, 2017. In the end, I wrote 10,680 words to produce a final draft of 2,803 words. Or, to put it another way, to find exactly the words I needed, I had to throw away 74% of what I wrote.

From my work I learned that writing lets me live my life twice – once when I experience it, and again later, when I try to make sense of it. I learned that if I put something down on the page, even if it's not quite right, I begin to remember things that I never would have remembered otherwise. For example, when I wrote about listening to a song at nine years old, I included in an early draft that I was a Cub Scout at the time. Without quite knowing why, I described my nine-year-old self as "loyal, thrifty, and brave." Later, after looking up the Cub Scout Promise, I changed the description to "loyal, thrifty, brave, clean, and reverent." Those are five of the twelve qualities listed in the promise, including the last three in order. Making this discovery through revision was important, because it let me hold off mentioning explicitly that I was a Cub Scout until later, when I wanted to emphasize that my parents always made sure that my brother and I were signed up for Cub Scouts and Little League.

The greatest obstacle I face now is finding a way to connect all of the essays that I have written (and the many more that I still need to write) into a coherent whole. Exploring my life through writing is like creating a mosaic or putting together a puzzle. While I work on the individual essays, it's difficult to see how they all fit together. I feel as though I'm at the point where I need a frame.

To overcome this problem, I will write an essay about a suggested topic that I found in a book of writing exercises: "Write about a place that is important to the history of who you have become." The point of the exercise is to describe a place so that the description reveals an attitude about the place. The working title of my essay is "The Heyday of the Yale Heights Boys' Club." It will try to recapture the feel of the streets and alleys and playgrounds and ball fields where I grew up dreaming of playing basketball and baseball for Mount Saint Joe.

By next Monday, I will have at least five one-page notebook entries about my memories of Yale Heights. These will include descriptions of places and people, the things that the people did in those places, and the times when they did them. I will also draw an 8 ½ x 11 annotated map from memory.

Résumé

Dan Peightel
472-2 Lambeth Commons
Charlottesville, VA 22901
834-4444

Objective:

To provide the support services that will help Virginia Basketball achieve its team goals.

Experience:

Head manager of Mount St. Joseph High School basketball team from 1976 – 1978.

Assistant manager of MSJ Gaels from 1974 – 1976.

Duties:

- Score keeping – during last two years, responsible for team's official scorebook

- Clock operation – during first two years, ran scoreboard clock for home games

- Charts & statistics – as asst. mgr., kept shot chart & other stats at away games

- Court maintenance – responsible for daily dust mopping of court

- Practice setup – made sure basketballs, towels, water were in place for practices

- Injury prevention – taped players' ankles before practice and games

- Injury treatment – assisted players with RICE (rest, ice, compression, elevation)

- Videotape recording – set up equipment for both recording and playback

- Road trip preparation – made sure everything packed, including extra shoelaces

Work History:

Summer 1979 – file clerk at the Register of Wills for Baltimore City

Summer 1978 – catalogue order associate at Montgomery Ward warehouse

Summer 1977 – grounds crew for Mount St. Joseph High School

School Year 1975–1978 – janitor for Mount St. Joseph High School gymnasium

May 1973 – August 1975 – delivery boy for the Baltimore Sun

Awards:

Ensign C. Markland Kelly Athletic Service Award – 1977 & 1978

Special Note: This sample résumé was originally formatted to fit on one side of standard 8 1/2 x 11 letterhead. It is formatted here to fit the pages of this text. Use this model as an example of how to show that your experience and skills make you the best candidate for the job. Your actual resume, however, must always fit on one page.

Confessions of a Shape Shifter
By Dan Peightel
(personal essay)

Last night, I aimed a Walther pistol at a defenseless man and shot him in the temple. Just before I pulled the trigger, he looked at me and said, "I surrender." But I shot him anyway.

At least this one had it coming.

Years ago, I murdered an old woman, a pawnbroker, just to see if I could get away with it. I surprised her in her apartment and bashed her skull with the blunt end of an axe. The sister returned home unexpectedly. I had no choice about her.

While still a young man, a war hero whose life might have gone differently, I murdered out of blind ambition. I betrayed my victim, stabbed him while he slept under my roof.

I have killed for revenge and called it justice. And I have killed for no reason at all, simply because a man was Arab and annoyed me.

But, for the moment, let's consider last night.

The Walther, side arm of German officers, has "a bare snout, like a Luger," but the barrel is shorter. When Degrave and I spotted the black Citroen following us on the treacherous mountain roads, I was grateful to have it tucked in my belt, "back where it couldn't be seen." The Citroen pulled ahead and stopped us outside of Beaufort-St.-Croix.

The leader, maybe nineteen, and the other two "all

wore armbands, white initials stitched on a blue field—
MF, for Milice Francaise." On patrol, they said. Fascist
thugs. They never suspected that we were carrying guns
beneath the cases of sardines stacked in that old truck.
They meant to steal our gasoline.

I have no idea "who shot first or why, but there
were five or six reports from the front of the truck." After
I shot the fat one sent back to check the cargo, I "edged
around the hood" until I could see the other side. By the
Citroen, the youngest one lay sprawled across a rifle, "his
blood a dark patch in the dirt."

In the front seat of the truck, Degrave was bleeding.
"We have to go," he said. "But first, make sure here." The
leader sat "with his back propped against the rear tire,
breathing hard, one hand inside his shirt." Just a boy. "The
report echoed over the fields and faded away."

How, you ask, could I have fought for the
Resistance in occupied France only last night? But I assure
you that I did.

Just as I skulked through the streets of Saint
Petersburg long ago, trying to avoid not just the inspector,
Porfiry Petrovich, but my own fevered conscience after
my foul deeds in the old woman's apartment.

Just as, after two future invasions of Earth, while
still a child, a prodigy of space warfare, I will sacrifice
hordes of my own fighters to slaughter the hated
"buggers"—only to find that I have been tricked by my
own commanders, and that the buggers have been
misunderstood.

I can travel not just great distances, but through

time. I live in the present, the past, and the future, all three. As keenly as I suffer the blazing Algerian sun on the day I murder the Arab, so I shiver against the shrewd, biting air on the ramparts of Elsinore and learn from the ghost that "time is out of joint" while Claudius reigns in Denmark.

I lose myself in pages and find selves I have not yet known. It's magic of the mind, the power of words to conjure worlds. The secret is in the details.

The "too sweet smell of wisteria blooming for the second time that summer" evokes "the biding and dreamy and victorious dust" of a "long still hot weary dead September afternoon." And, inexorably, I am Quentin Compson, riding out in a buggy with Miss Rosa Coldfield to discover, long after dark of that same September night, the family secrets that compelled Henry Sutpen to murder his sister's fiancé, Charles Bon, at the very gates of Sutpen's Hundred, tangled secrets of race and repudiation, pride and sin and sorrow, ending finally, culminating, in conflagration and defeat.

On another night, I am beaten half to death and nearly have my throat slit by an invisible man. His invisibility, it turns out, comes not from his black skin, but from "a peculiar disposition of the eyes" of those who "see only [his] surroundings, themselves, or figments of their imagination—indeed, everything and anything except [him]." Angry and exhausted from playing roles others expect of him, he "hibernates" in a New York City manhole illuminated with energy stolen from Monopolated Light & Power. I follow him down and listen to him explain Louis Armstrong's "What Did I Do to Be So Black and Blue."

You may think me a liar, a hipster, a trickster, a shape shifter. But I have lived underground and had my eyes opened to the truth of invisibility. From my many lives, I know more than I hear from the network news. From imagined experience, I know that the lonely perpetrator of the latest mall shooting, though his deeds are monstrous, is more than just a monster.

"All happy families are alike," Tolstoy tells us. "Each unhappy family is unhappy in its own way." The mall shooter was a human being, a kid from a family more or less happy. And echoing the Roman playwright Terrence I say, "Nothing human is alien to me."

I seek always to enlarge my soul, to expand my capacity for empathy. I seek to know how others live. And how they die.

"To philosophize," Montaigne says, "is to prepare to die."

In still another of my lives, "humping the boonies" with First Lieutenant Jimmy Cross, I ambushed a man walking down a trail. Afterwards, lying there, blown out of his rubber sandals, "his one eye was shut, his other eye was a star-shaped hole . . . there was a butterfly on his chin, his neck was open to the spinal cord and the blood there was thick and shiny and it was this wound that had killed him." From his small, frail appearance, I imagined that he had "wanted someday to be a teacher of mathematics." The hard truth is each of us dies alone. We are, each of us, estranged from ourselves. Killing, even to save the world, costs us pieces of our humanity. Stories open us to the possibility of a self like our own in each stranger we meet. Like me, the Arab whom I murdered also sought to make meaning of a life under the blazing Algerian sun. I read to understand the darkness within me, to confront the darkness within us all.

Dreams and Obligations
By Dan Peightel
(memoir)

Back when I dreamt of growing up to be both Neil Armstrong and Brooks Robinson, my father treasured a few extra dollars and a free Friday or Saturday night to spend in the darkroom making prints. As a Field Engineer for Burroughs Corporation, he often worked double shifts installing computerized check sorters at Maryland National Bank.

One evening, with the dogwood in bloom, and plenty of daylight left for hitting grounders, he lugged his attaché case from the car and plunked it next to the desk by the living room stairs. As he dumped his cigarettes and lighter and keys on the desk, I said "Hey, Dad."

He didn't even hear me. After trudging upstairs for a nap, he came to supper grumbling about Ostrander and Johnson and Shope, names without faces. They wanted him to go to Detroit. For training. On the 6700.

"Twelve weeks?" my mother said. "That's the whole summer."

She claimed not to see why he couldn't just tell them no. He pushed his plate away and lit a cigarette. Joe and I were both in Catholic school. That was why. And the water heater might go up in a month.

Outside, Skeeter barked at kids spinning out their Big Wheels in the alley. "Knock it off," my father growled toward the screen door.

Pushing around the smoked neck and Brussels

sprouts on my plate, I summoned the courage to ask him about hitting some grounders. He crushed his cigarette in the ashtray and said, "I'm kind of tired tonight, pal."

I turned to my mother. "Finish your potatoes and go shoot some baskets," she said. "Maybe Dad'll come out in a little while."

Five minutes later, the kitchen door opened.

My father and I shot H-O-R-S-E until dark, barely saying a word, except to call backboard, or swish, or a trick shot.

Holt, Ratliff, and Reese
By Dan Peightel

for Chuck Thompson,
who taught me free verse
when I was ten

Killebrew walks.
    And the bases
        are loaded.

The sub, Mrs. Freeman,
    let us put away
        our long division.
We hunched forward
    and stared at her
        plastic transistor radio.
Better than the Twins,
    we wanted to forget
        the year before,
when we were better
    than Swoboda and Agee
        and the Amazin' Mets.

Now the two strike offering.
    Palmer ready.
        Here it is—
Struck him out.
    Swing-and-a-miss.
        Holt goes down.

And Palmer
      turned that one
            loose.

The zip on *loose*
      caught the corner
          of my memory,
sent me trudging
      back to the bench
         again,
Mom-mom calling,
      "It's okay, Bunk—
         Get 'em next time!"
Holt would shake his head,
      glance back at the mound,
             down at his shoes,
into far right field,
      anywhere to avoid
         the accusing, fearful
eyes of his teammates.
      Mrs. Freeman, walking
         up and down the aisles,
stopped at my desk
      and smiled.
         "You really pay attention,
every pitch."
      I flushed, and listened hard
         to pick up the new count.

The battle between Palmer

and Paul Ratliff
now standing
at two balls, two strikes.
Palmer kicks and throws—
Curved him. Strike
three is called.
And no comment
from Ratliff.

A valiant enemy, Ratliff
lost no dignity in defeat,
bore his fate
like "tall Hector
of the shining helmet"
in the *Iliad*
Ms. Benner read to us
before she left
on her honeymoon.
One whole afternoon
she read and reread
Hector's farewell
to Andromache,
even skipped math,
trying to show us
it wasn't all
blood and guts
and battles.
"Even as 'Victory passes
back and forth between men,'
the poet

takes time to see,
    to tell us about,
        character."

Now another
    dangerous left-handed swinger,
        Rich Reese.

Quickly, Palmer had him
    in a hole, nothing and two.
        But then Reese ripped
a line drive
    foul down the line,
        and Palmer missed
high and outside.
    "Tough with two,"
        Dad always called
in this spot.
    "Anything close."
        Reese heard him,
and chipped just
    a piece of two
        on the fists,
and two more
    just off the corner.
        Desks tilted forward
and thumped back,
    with each one
        Palmer wasted
high and tight,

and even Mrs. Freeman
    forgot her warning about it.
Reese fought off
    another—ground it
        foul just off first.

And another.

And again we'll have
    the three-two pitch.
Palmer set.
    The runners go.
        The pitch.
Strike
    three
        called!
Palmer,
    with a brilliant comeback,
        struck out
Holt,
    Ratliff,
        and Reese.
At the end of three-and-a-half,
    it's Baltimore five,
        Minnesota nothing.

I heard American poetry
    before I knew Whitman
        or Williams or the Beats,
heard it

in the prepositional phrase
prolonging the moment,
heard it
in the pronunciation
of the three names

like three
untouchable pitches
popping in a mitt,
heard it
in the falling cadence
and the final click
closing the inning
that closed the door
on the Twins.

But it was more
than the occasion,
more than the magical
combination of consonants
and curveballs. It was
all the innings called.
It was every
routine putout
in Cleveland in July.

Slow roller,
third-base line.
Brooks charges,
barehanded pickup,

the long throw—
        In time!

The promise of poetry
        (and its demand) for
                a no-stick daydreamer
was this openness
        to the ordinary,
                yet readiness for
the sensational,
        this daily practice
                of the particular.

"No ideas
        but in things."
                Indeed.

Ain't
        the beer
                cold!

Because a Man Served God
By Dan Peightel
(multi-voice free verse poem)

Because Br. James never let
the faculty begin a year without
a reminder to take care
of the snot-nosed, pimply-faced
fat kid who gets pushed
into lockers, my teacher saw
behind my smudged glasses
the light in my eyes, heard
in my stammer the poems
I wanted to write and the lectures
I give today to my own classes.

Because forty years ago Br. James
visited my Junior Retreat and told
about the difficulty of forgiving
his father and the difficulty
of asking forgiveness in return,
I forgave my own father
leaving us, and loved
my youngest son when,
no longer proud and prodigal,
but bruised and battered by life,
he came home from rehab.

Because Br. James stood
by his pillar every day and waited

for us to say hello, I learned
the importance of eye contact
and a simple greeting, I learned
the importance of reliability,
of showing up each day ready
to pay attention to the world
around me. Though he never
taught me in class and struggled
to remember my name, I learned
the meaning of caring.

Because Br. James hauled me
into his office and chewed me out
for turning in a paper full of B.S.,
I began to take my work seriously,
to take advantage of the gifts
he saw in me, to want at first
to please him, and later
to be pleased with nothing less
than my best. Because of Br. James
I learned the importance of commas,
and I learned to love learning.

Because Br. James apologized
for blowing his stack unfairly
at our Brit. Lit. class, I learned
that even good men sin, and
that we must all make amends.
I learned that honesty requires
more than saying whatever's

on your mind. Real honesty
requires the willingness
to admit when you're wrong.

Because Br. James began every
Monday morning with a pep talk,
I knew that when a pigeon pooped
on my head I should wear my seatbelt.
And soon after the start of senior year
I acted like I would "do nothing"
between then and graduation.
But deep down, I learned
that giving blood is a Christic act,
that I should be careful not
to fall in with the wrong crowd,
and that it's my job to look out
for the Eddies of the world.
And way down, in my soul,
where I wouldn't forget,
I understood how much I wanted
never to break my mother's heart.

Because Br. James began every
class, every meal, every day,
every act, "In the name
of the Father, and the Son,
and the Holy Spirit," because
he reminded us to perform
every action for the love of God,
I remember to pray for help

and to pray in thanksgiving.

Because Br. James talked bluntly
about the details of his illness,
I believed him when he talked
about the "privilege" of sharing
in Christ's passion, and I found
the grace to accept my suffering,
to find in it the promise
of redemption. I found
the courage to act with faith
even when my faith was weak,
the courage to truly acknowledge
my own mortality, the courage
to believe that what matters
is not my death, but how I live.

Because in 2001 Br. James listened
to the entreaties of a friend since college
and heard in them the call of God,
because against all reason he left
the comfort of a life in Louisville
and came to the Mount, because
he had the wisdom to nurture dreams
and the integrity to say no
to fond dreams when necessary,
because he refused to defer maintenance
and thought often of his responsibility
to me, "some future headmaster,"
because – relying on the great St. Joseph –

he was unafraid to humbly ask
on behalf of the boys, because –
always – Brother James marched on,
I will this afternoon, in the Cathedral
of his beloved Virgin Mary,
hand diplomas to boys not even born in 2011,
to boys become men, men who matter.

A Wedding Vow
By Dan Peightel
(sonnet)

You see with a novelist's eye and love
with a poet's wounded heart. The earthquakes
you've stood have cleared the ground for us. Above
the drone each day, your bright two-note laugh wakes
my ego from its worthless worry. Do
my words and feeble gestures indicate
at all the deep respect I hold for you,
my deep desire to be a worthy mate?
I love the love in all the homework fights
we wage as one. I love each bigger test
we face, demands that bring such rich delights.
I know that I am so divinely blessed.
I promise to keep God's gifts in my heart,
to nourish sympathy, love's tender art.

In the Art Room—And Beyond
By Dan Peightel
(report of a visit / profile of an enterprise)

During the first period of a Wednesday morning, with the Art Room bathed in the soft north light that artists treasure, eight students from Advanced Drawing and Painting gather in a loose semicircle for "critique day." Pins hold eight charcoal and chalk still-life drawings on a display board. Some of the drawings are on white paper, some on black, and some on ivory. Each student chose his own subject and created his own composition. Each has a stake in the coming discussion.

Perched on a stool off to the side, Mr. Ken Pittman moderates an unhurried discussion that evolves out of the students' observations. A drawing on ivory paper of a cut-glass lamp, a candlestick, and a pewter goblet lying on its side between them elicits a number of positive comments from the group.

"It's realistic," one student says. "You can see he put a lot of time on it." Another student elaborates. "I like the reflections of the glass. He did a good job with the curves." After the initial rush, a brief quiet settles. As they think, Pittman points out that the artist used a daring technique to draw the goblet. "Eliminating all of the middle tone usually doesn't work. But in this case it does, because we believe the cup is pewter."

The discussion moves on to some of the other drawings. One of a baseball cap earns praise for its strong light source and the way the fold in the cap gives it texture.

Another, on black paper, of a cup, some bottles and cans, and a tape measure seems crowded. Pittman suggests that the artist "push the objects in front a little bit harder," shade them heavier with the white chalk, to create more space and shadow between them and the object behind.

Over the course of twenty minutes, all eight drawings receive attention. Pittman, who concentrated in Art Teacher Education while earning his MFA from the Maryland Institute College of Art, brings the discussion back to the first drawing, using a minor weakness in the best piece to teach a lesson about "elliptical conflict" for them all. "The base of the lamp isn't as open as the base of the candlestick," he says. "It works out okay, because most of it's concealed by the mouth of the cup. But that one corner isn't quite as open as it could be."

With half an hour left in the period, Pittman turns his students loose to work on their individual oil paintings. They talk quietly, about their projects and about other topics, as they take out their materials. Some move off to distant corners of the room. But all set about their work with no need of reminder from the teacher.

Over by the kiln, junior Aaron LeKarz works on a painting of a peregrine falcon perched on the ledge of a skyscraper. He wants the painting to symbolize openness, freedom, and majesty. Today he concentrates on establishing exactly the right background sky. "I want it to feel almost like a self-portrait of an animal."

LeKarz thrives in an atmosphere where assignments

serve as helpful guidelines rather than tight restrictions. He often comes to the Art Room to work during his free periods. "We start new projects just for the fun of it," he says. "And whenever we finish something, we go straight into something else."

At an easel a few feet from LeKarz, sophomore David Badalato works on an oil painting that he began three months ago. The original inspiration came from a photograph taken on a family vacation at Mrytle Beach. During the course of the work, however, he has eliminated a house and chosen to focus just on the power of the waves crashing on shore.

Like LeKarz, Badalato enjoys the atmosphere in the Art Room. He attributes that to Pittman's skill as a teacher. "He actually knows something," Badalato says. He appreciates Pittman's ability to demonstrate techniques. "It really helps when you get stuck."

But the creative atmosphere fostered by this class is not confined just to the Art Room. Each year the Advanced Painting and Drawing crew completes a mural somewhere around campus. Past members of this class have painted a space exploration mural for the Xavier Hall computer lab, an arrangement of Keith Haring-style outline figures playing musical instruments for the band room, and a sunset vista framed by classical stone columns and arches for Room 1, a windowless basement classroom.

This year, the group meets every B-day in Room 2 of the Fine Arts Center for "mural day." Mr. Zeiger teaches a freshman English class in the same room during this period. "I'm amazed," he says. "If you had asked me before we started, I would have said it couldn't work. But Ken's got about a dozen kids in there working and I'm able to teach my class with no distractions. We haven't had a single incident."

Pittman chose a Monet-inspired scene of a pond lush with lily pads and wild flowers as the subject of the mural. "The goal is to brighten the environment," he says. "What we're putting up there is actually a composite from studies drawn by the kids."

The students divide work according to their own choice. Pittman recommends that they move around so that various styles and brush techniques blend throughout the mural. Lately LeKarz has worked on the reflections of trees in the pond. "The challenge is to match colors that others are using," he says. "Water has no color. It reflects. But ripples in the water distort things. The actual trees look definite. Their reflections look faded."

Badalato also likes to concentrate on the water. But he has only worked on the mural two or three times. As a sophomore, he misses some classes because he must take Phys. Ed. every other day. Although he will play defense on this year's J.V. lacrosse team, he prefers art to gym class. "No question," he says. "I'd rather be working on the mural. Definitely."

In the Line of Duty
By Dan Peightel
(profile / family history)

     In June of 1960, two months before I was born, my grandfather, Charles "Bud" Ernest, shot and killed a man on Edmondson Avenue. In the midst of a running battle through the streets of west Baltimore, a suspect in an attempted assault on a woman aimed his gun at the turned head of my grandfather's partner. Although the suspect had previously fired three shots at my grandfather, it was only when his partner's life was threatened that my grandfather fired his first shot.

     About a year prior to that shooting, my grandfather had escaped injury in another one. But his temporary partner, Officer James J. Purcell, was killed. Purcell had jumped out of the radio car in front of the house to which they had been called, and my grandfather drove around to cover the back. As Purcell went up the steps, a man came out the front door shooting. "Bud was really busted up about that," my grandmother says. "He was a pallbearer at the funeral."

     Loyalty drove my grandfather. He learned about it up close as a rifleman in 1st Platoon, Company E, of the 158th Regimental Combat Team. Known as the Bushmasters, the 158th cut its combat teeth on New Guinea in March 1944. A year later, as part of the American Sixth Army, the Bushmasters invaded the Bicol Peninsula in southern Luzon. By the time they landed at Legaspi on April 1, Easter Sunday, 1945, MacArthur's forces had already captured Manila and all the strategic objectives in the Philippines. My grandfather and his friends were left to root out and destroy the Japanese forces, who fought a torturous delaying action through mountainous jungle.

"There were few major clashes," according to Geoffrey Perret's *There's A War to Be Won.* "Instead, there was a seemingly endless round of firefights that, in a typical division, would

kill and seriously wound 30 to 40 men a day" (513). Sometime in mid-April, as they advanced mile-by-mile and yard-by-yard toward Naga, grenade shrapnel tore into my grandfather's back and he became one of a day's statistics.

He sent home some pictures taken at a field hospital in Legaspi on April 25, 1945. In one, he mugs for the camera beneath heavy facial bandages, while one of his buddies pretends to check him with a stethoscope. A hand-written note on the back reads, "That is me all patched up like that just for the fun of it. I wasn't in that bad a shape when I was in the hospital as you can see by the other pictures."

In the most poignant of those other pictures, he stands second from the right in a group of four guys on a muddy street between rows of hospital tents. No one in the group is identified. My grandfather and two of the others wear pajamas and combat boots. The fourth young man, in khaki fatigues, smokes a cigar. Perhaps his visit from their unit has provided the occasion for the pictures.

They are safe for the moment, out of enemy

artillery range, but unsure of what awaits them. If anyone's recovery takes longer than thirty days, he will be considered a "casual," a replacement who can be sent anywhere. They stand joined at the hip, arms draped around each other's shoulders and waists. If they have to go back into action, they want to go with their buddies.

More than twenty police officers arrived on the scene the night of my grandfather's gun battle on Edmondson Avenue. According to the *Baltimore News-Post*, as my grandfather pursued the fleeing suspect, the man fired a fifth shot. "Patrolman Ernest then shot three times and the man hid between two parked cars." Those few moments must have seemed a lifetime—trying to spot the suspect, trying to make an arrest, having to shoot a man at close range.

After the first shot at my grandfather, radio cars rushed to the scene. But no one else fired a shot. Most of the others arrived after the suspect lay dead. I can barely imagine the mixture of fear and rage that must have swirled through my grandfather as he faced death alone in the dark. In the end, he had no choice. According to the *News-Post*, "Ernest fired his fifth shot, hitting the man in the face."

Whenever I would ask my mother about the incident, she would claim not to remember very much about it. Her standard answer was to joke about what a blunderer my grandfather's partner was. "Somebody always had to watch out for Dietz," she would say. "His number just wasn't up that day." She maintained that my grandfather, quiet by nature, never brought the job home with him. "Pop-pop got put on desk duty for a couple of days, but that was about it. He never really said much about it."

My grandfather died on January 20, 1965. Six months earlier, while taking a report from one driver involved in a traffic accident, he instructed the other driver to move his car from the intersection. The man later claimed that, when he attempted to do so, the gearshift stuck in reverse. Some witnesses thought that he meant to flee the scene. The force of the blow threw my grandfather above the telephone wires.

Still on crutches in January, he faced a third operation and the prospect of never again walking normally. At a hearing after his death, a police department doctor testified that stress, combined with the broken hip and the physical exertion of hauling himself around on crutches, led to his fatal heart attack. The department ruled his death "in the line of duty."

My grandfather lived an ordinary life punctuated by moments of incredible violence. But he never thought of himself as a hero. He would have been uncomfortable with anyone calling him that. Whether lying wounded in the mud on Luzon or standing over the body of a man who shot at him, Charlie Ernest was just doing the job that had to be done. It was no more heroic than filling out a report.

Learning to See
By Dan Peightel
Published in *The Baltimore Review*
(essay)

The calm of the group's leader draws me to the photograph. Squatting on the edge of an Inner Harbor dock timber, knees up almost to his shoulders, he leans forward, out over the water, to work his crab line. The wet line tugs against his dirty fingers as he lets it drift. The trick is to let the crab come to the chicken neck, to let it sink its pincer deep in the meat, then to draw steadily, never letting the crab feel the pull of the current. It's like filching Hershey bars from the five-and-dime. When the boy concentrates, he can slow his heart beat.

My father took the photograph at Pier 5, across from the Baltimore Gas & Electric power plant, in 1954. When I was a kid, the framed print hung amid several others on the knotty pine wall of our club basement. Every week, when I dusted all the frames, I searched the picture's details, hoping—I think now—to understand how my father saw the world.

The younger brother of the leader sits safely to his right on the same timber. The younger boy knows better than to ape the older one's daredevil stance. That would mean a smack and a warning from the older boy, or—worse—ridicule from one of his side-kicks. The younger boy also knows better than to ask for help. His line lies slimy and tangled in his lap. He works to recast, glad for the older boy's attention to his own line.

My father grew up with four younger siblings. His room was at the top front of a rented three-story rowhouse at 2330 North Charles Street. The five kids shared a hallway bathroom with no windows. By stuffing towels between the door and the threshold, he could turn it into a makeshift darkroom. Still learning his craft back then, he cost himself more chemicals and paper than he could really afford. But this negative was special. I imagine his sisters pounding on the locked door, imagine him reprinting the picture until he was sure it would breathe and speak.

The older brother's two-tone canvas shoes mark him as the leader. The two boys to his left wear scuffed black oxfords. Their mothers would never go for shoes so impractical, shoes that wouldn't last a whole school year. The two sidekicks know he'll punch whoever's handy when he spots the first mark on his new kicks. But they can't figure out why, three months from now, when the white insteps have turned greasy black, he won't care that his little toe pushes through the canvas.

Even in postwar prosperity, my father's mother sometimes had to feed her kids ketchup sandwiches. Her husband's dreams of bigger commissions and his sharp tongue with bosses meant starting over too many times to get ahead. She had little left over to encourage her son's hobby. Still, my father would show her every new batch of prints. With Terry, his two-year-old brother, on her lap, she'd flip through them, while the twins, Connie and Carol Anne, bickered upstairs. When she came to the photograph of the boys crabbing, she said, "This one's not bad."

The boy at the center of the photograph is the only one who might snare a crab. When he quits, they'll all toss away their lines and follow. The heavyset boy, seated on the granite curb to which the timber is bolted, leans out over the water too, but with a plodding, fumbler's center of gravity. He resents, in ways he has no words to express, the élan of the leader. He senses already that he'll never get the same kind of girls.

Back then, my father was rail thin, nothing but knobs and sharp angles. He wore a crew cut and eyeglasses with black GI frames. He never knew quite what to say to the girls in the youth group at Lovely Lane Methodist Church. But when they were in the mood, they'd beg him to take their picture. They'd laugh and pose for him, flirt with his camera.

The boy in the polka dot shirt spots the photographer advancing his film. "Hey, mister!" the boy calls out. "Take our picture." He sits the curb sidesaddle, hips turned, knees together. As always, he watches intently, remembers all that happens. But it's not really his memory that counts. He gets to hang around because he tells the stories best, creates the memories the other boys want to have.

The leader has never looked up from his line. But now he says, "You work for the newspaper, mister?" He possesses more than know how, more even than confidence. He possesses himself, possesses the moment if not the future. He doesn't know that forty-five years down the line his pension from Bethlehem Steel or his health care benefits from GM will be stolen from him. He can't imagine that in the blink of an eye his brother might be strung out on fear and dope, fighting for his life in a meaningless place called Khe Sahn.

The photographer balances on the dock timber to take his light reading, set f-stop and shutter speed. Only seventeen, he lets the question hang in the air, lets the smart aleck think what he wants. The light is perfect, cloudy bright. Alive to the moment's passing, the photographer leans out over the water. His Rolleicord hangs from a leather strap around his neck. He sharpens the focus. An instant before squeezing the shutter, he holds his breath.

Afterwards he will smoke a cigarette, a Winston. Imagining that teenager with a camera, I glimpse an adding machine repairman who will photograph weddings on Saturdays to earn extra money. And I glimpse a family man, newly promoted, who will turn down an attractive job with F. Paul Galeone Studios, because there's more future in computer repair. In that lean, laconic high school student, looking around so intently for another picture, I can almost see my father.

Music Out of Baltimore
By Dan Peightel
(essay)

The Bullets game blared from the plastic RCA radio on my father's workbench. He wanted to hear it in the darkroom. "Wes down low. Out to Earl. Drives baseline. Fifteen footer. Bulls-eye!"

We loved the staccato style of Jim Karvellas. The year before, my father had taken Joe and me to the Civic Center for a playoff game against the Knicks. But the thrill now of each "Bulls-eye!" on the radio was almost as good.

As the game see-sawed, Joe and I raced slot cars on the track that my father set up special with the Christmas decorations each year. Now that we were back to school, my mother would want the decorations and the racecars packed away soon. But she was out at a meeting to plan her Seton class reunion. Miss Dolores, my godmother, had picked her up.

In the end, the Bullets won a close one. This year, I said, we'd show the Knicks. "I don't know," my father said. "They're pretty good." Then he asked if I would bring him a coffee. I had done it before, but my mother had always been in the kitchen to pour it.

Upstairs, I mixed in sugar and milk until the coffee turned caramel, the way she had shown me. Perfect. Except on each step I had to stop and let it settle. When I sat it on his workbench, he was moving a print to the wash tray. He asked if we wanted to stay up and listen to Harley. "He usually plays jazz," he said. "But tonight it's all

Johnny Cash."

I hadn't told my father, hadn't told anybody, that Billy Pomasano and Mike Manic made fun of me that past summer when they found out we watched *The Johnny Cash Show*. Long-haired and barefoot, a few years older than I was, they had perched on a backyard fence just across the alley while I tossed pop-ups to myself. "What?" they said. "Is that who your father likes?"

Now, following Galen Fromme with the eleven o'clock headlines on WBAL, came the grumbling trombones of Duke Ellington's "Things Ain't What They Used to Be." And then a voice full of gravel and cigarettes. "It's the Harley Show, music out of Baltimore." That night's program started with "Folsom Prison." But then Harley went back to the early days, with rambling stories between Johnny's rockabilly hits. My father shushed us.

Harley Brinsfield loved and lived music. In the old days, according to my father, Harley had known and been good to Billie Holiday. But this night he had bills to pay. After a Cash set ending with "Ring of Fire," he hawked the Harley Burger and the Harley Original. My father has always been a night owl, attracted to bright lights and coffee shops and hamburger joints. "When your mother gets back," he said. "We'll go get us a Harley Burger. With extra sauce."

Of course, when she came in, she wanted to know what we were doing up. We told her about Johnny Cash. "You have to get up early," she said. "We've got a lot to do, grocery shopping and the tree and the decorations." We promised we'd get up. But she was really talking to my father. That's when we asked about Harley's.

"Please, Mom. Please," we said. My father tucked the last of the prints in a blotter roll and washed his trays. Finally my mother said that, if my father thought we could afford it, she guessed, this one time, it would be all right. But not every Friday.

We piled into our yellow Plymouth Valiant. The heater fought a losing battle against the cold rushing in the driver's vent triangle, open for my father's cigarette. "It's in a new development," my mother said. She was talking about her classmate Enid's house. "And Dolores says Bob wants to look up near Eldersburg."

At Harley's on Route 40 near Ingleside, next to the Westview Fairlanes, my father sent me and Joe in with the order. "Extra sauce," he said. The tinkling bell above the door roused the only other customer, a long-haired man in an army jacket who had been dosing in the fluorescent light. The wrinkled lady at the register said nothing when I told her extra sauce. Joe and I sat at the opposite end of a row of orange plastic chairs from the man in the army jacket. Behind the counter a woman with stringy hair, maybe the gruff woman's daughter, scraped the grill with a metal spatula. I clenched the ten dollar bill in my coat pocket and hoped my parents were keeping an eye on us.

When we got back in the warm car, the night was different. The volume on the radio was turned up, and my parents, sitting with space between them, looking out opposite windows, listened to Johnny and June sing "Jackson." My father stubbed out another cigarette and released the parking brake.

Off and on over the next several years, my mother would bring up moving. They'd wonder whether saving what they paid in tuition at the Monastery, and later the $800 a year at St. Joe, would be enough. They'd talk about sending us to Sykesville Middle and then to South Carroll, where the Trumpler kids went to school after they left Yale Heights.

Harley's dead. And the Harley Burger is long gone. The Bullets, and even the Colts, left Baltimore. But my father still stays up late making prints. Digital now, it's true. But still in that same knotty pine basement on Wickham Road, listening to music and drinking coffee.

A Sunday in January 2010
By Dan Peightel
(prose poem)

In the living room this morning, a rhombus of sunlight fell on our polished oak floor. The shadow of a carved chair arm bespoke comfort amid recession, luxury, if also unease. Outside, snow frosted the tops of barren branches. In the brittle air, we shoveled clean our parking places, scraped windshields today to save time tomorrow, laughed with our neighbor, forgot for a moment her chemo and, already, the orphans of Haiti.

Always Splitting the Dark
By Dan Peightel
(personal essay)

When I graduated from the Mount in 1978, I had my whole life mapped out in the caption under my yearbook picture. "Next year Dan will attend UVA and after graduation he plans to enroll in the University's law school." But my future changed during my second year of college, when I had to stay in Charlottesville with the basketball team over Christmas break.

All semester I had been reading required texts on political theory, and legal history, and economics. I wanted a story. By chance, I picked up Robert Penn Warren's *All the King's Men*, a book I was supposed to read for AP English but never did. On page thirty-six, the narrator, Jack Burden, describes a midnight ride he takes with his boss, Willie Stark, the governor of Louisiana.

"Close to the road a cow would stand knee-deep in the mist, with horns damp enough to have a pearly shine in the starlight and would look at the black blur we were as we went whirling into the blazing corridor of light which we could never quite get into for it would be always splitting the dark just in front of us."

The vividness of the light in that sentence stunned me. Years earlier, riding home in the back seat of our car late at night, unable to make sense of my parents' hushed conversation about the people we'd been visiting, I'd mesmerized myself trying to freeze the shadows cast on the seatback by the headlights of cars coming up from behind.

Now, in my apartment in Charlottesville, I lay the book face down on my chest and stared at the blank white ceiling. I wanted to render my experience in sentences that would stop people this way. I wanted to make pictures with words.

Ever since then, I've been trying to figure out what I have to say. I know it has something to do with the husband and wife in the front seat of that car, and with the little brother asleep beside the boy trying to freeze the shadows. With what they were talking about, what they feared, and what they dreamed was possible.

It has to do with dissatisfaction. With credit card debt and health insurance and tuition. And with hope and hard work. With growing up in Yale Heights and listening to Chuck and wanting to be Brooks. With striking out thirty-one straight times my first year in Little League, and with my grandmother saying all I needed was confidence.

It has to do with arguments, and with words of anger that went unspoken. With small kindnesses, and words of love spoken out of habit. With Cub Scouts, and science fair projects, and wrestling the Christmas tree into the stand every year. It has to do with places—Saint Joe, and City College, and the old Seton High School, with the Monastery and the Kozy Klub and the Double T, with Yale Bowl and Slentz's Field and Matt's yard.

It also has to do with larger, public concerns—with crime and racism, property values and politics, with sports franchises and stadiums and schools. It has to do with history—with Kitty Delahanty facing down the pastor of

Fourteen Holy Martyrs who came to complain about her dollar-apiece card readings; with a wounded Charlie Ernest lying all night in the mud on Luzon, terrified of a Japanese bayonet attack; with Amos Peightel disappointing his son (my father) by supporting the segregationist Orval Faubus against nine black school children in Little Rock.

It has to do with family, with the tension between responsibility and the pursuit of happiness. And, one character at a time, it has to do with the fundamental question of our dying world: Can nonviolence confront hatred and win?

One character at a time, and one place at a time. That's the value of literature. Students have often asked me, "Why do we have to read this?" It's a good question. One that deserves a better answer than, "Because we say so." Literature isn't written by dead guys. Nobody writes Literature (with a capital L). Living, breathing, loving, sinning people write stories, trying to make sense of what they've done or haven't done, whom they've loved and how they've hated.

These stories—and poems, plays, essays, and memoirs—are worth reading even after the writers have died, because they bring to life, in a specific time and place, what William Faulkner called "the human heart in conflict with itself." I hope this class has shown you not only why literature is worth reading, but also that you can write it.

Literature is about you. It's about the enormous emotion that attaches to a moment only you remember: a dispute over meld in a game of 500 Rummy, and your father's insinuation that you tried to cheat. You imagine it again, smell the kerosene from the lamp on the campsite picnic table, slap the mosquito on the back of your neck. You observe your own sadness when your stepson turns over the board and ruins what started out as a pleasant game of checkers. All of it leads you to write a story about a son not able to understand a father's pain as a grandmother dies of breast cancer.

It may take you longer than you ever expected to find the skill to make people see. And it may never pay you a dime. But the work is worth the doing. What you have to say emerges from the struggle to say it—emerges like sculpture from the stone. You may never freeze those shadows, or enter that blazing corridor of light, but at least you can sometimes split the dark in front of you.

At the Hour of Our Death
By Dan Peightel
(personal essay)

When I suffered an episode of sudden cardiac arrest in August 2006, Brother James had already endured his initial bout with cancer. On my first day back at school, he paused in the hallway to ask how I was doing. "You've had a brush with your own mortality," he said. "You're bound to see things differently."

Back then, I thought I knew what he meant. We both understood something that other people didn't. Or so his certainty seemed to imply. Now, however, I wonder what else he might have said if I'd asked him to elaborate. I wonder if he was offering me a chance to talk.

But that wasn't really our relationship. He was the boss. So, except for business, we stuck to formal pleasantries. When he paced the portico with his Dictaphone, we would simply exchange a nod. Even in the last few months of his life, he worked as hard as he could. And I felt as though he expected more from me than chit-chat.

Our only remotely philosophical exchanges occurred through e-mail. In April of 2010, I wrote to him about *Disrupting Class*, a study by three Harvard Business School professors, which predicts that by 2019 "disruptive deployment" of computers will "flip" the market for high school education, much the way the iPod and iTunes have flipped the market for music. I wanted him to see the wonders.

The next morning he wrote back. "I have no doubt that you are right and that these changes will come about." But he wasn't thrilled. "For my part, I thank God that I'll probably be in the Old Brothers' Home by 2019." And he went on to say why. "My joy in teaching over the last 40 years has come from the personal contact with the kids."

At first I wanted to point out that computers can increase personal attention. But then I realized that Brother already knew that. His objections arose from within. "I'm not a man who would learn well in an on-line course," he wrote. "And I don't think I'm one who would do well teaching such a course."

Later in 2010, just after school ended in June, a bunch of us on the faculty traded e-mail about what we planned to read for the summer. At the end of my list, I mentioned *Stoner*, the best novel I had read in the past five years. On the very first page, the author tells us the facts of William Stoner's birth, death, and unremarkable life. "Stoner's colleagues, who held him in no particular esteem when he was alive, speak of him rarely now; to the older ones, his name is a reminder of the end that awaits them all, and to the younger ones it is merely a sound which evokes no sense of the past and no identity with which they can associate themselves or their careers." Yet the story of Stoner's life makes a spell-binding novel.

Brother was part of the e-mail exchange. But he had no intention of reading *Stoner*, or anything else on my list. "I'm in the middle of the memoirs of General Lord

Ismay," he wrote. Lord Ismay had been Churchill's chief of staff. And next up was Joyce Grenfell, "an English comedian, songstress and actress," who entertained the troops during World War II. "Keeping with my passion for reading memoirs, I have ordered everything Joyce wrote and will be plowing through it this summer." Like all avid readers, Brother felt the press of time. "I need to read more things which are modern, but memoirs fascinate me."

In the last weeks of Brother's life, I thought again of our brief e-mail exchanges and of the novel *Stoner*. I wished that Brother had gotten time to read that book. He would have recognized in it, I think, a kind of old-fashioned integrity. He would have appreciated its celebration of the enormous and noble effort required to do what little one can do.

On the book's last page, the dying professor experiences a "kind of joy," and all thoughts of failure seem "unworthy of what his life had been." Stoner's bedside table is piled with books, including his own forgotten work. Reaching out for his book, he knows that he won't find himself "in that fading print," yet a small part of him is there "and would be there."

At the November meeting during which Brother announced to the faculty that he would no longer be coming to school every day, he reminded us that the Mount would go on, would thrive, without him. "We are, all of us, useful but not necessary," he said. "I have been useful. But I am not necessary."

In Professor Stoner's final moment, death comes

not as a threat to be resisted, but as a hard-won peace, a respite from worry and pretense. "A sense of his own identity came upon him with a sudden force, and he felt the power of it. He was himself, and he knew who he had been." At the hour of our death, we should each hope to be so blessed.

Since being resuscitated five plus years ago, I have sought to make my extra days count. But too often I am not who I want to be. I eat too much junk and exercise too little. I anesthetize myself with TV and gadgets and trips to the mall. I stupidly put off visiting my parents, and I pretend that work will save me.

Rarely have I known anyone who was more himself, or knew better who he had been, than Brother James. Often now, as I muddle through a last-period class, a dull paragraph, I try to imagine what more Brother might have said about confronting our own mortality. The answer, like his Monday morning pep talks, always comes phrased in the imperative. "Live now the way you want to be remembered. Think about that. Live the way you want to be remembered. And learn to ask for forgiveness."

Back with Bud
By Dan Peightel
A Eulogy for Dorothy M. Ernest
March 13, 1922 – August 10, 2007

For those of you who don't know me, I'm Bunk.

That's how my grandmother always greeted me. "Hey, Bunk."

If you've ever seen an episode of *Homicide* or *The Wire*, you know that Bunk is what a good Baltimore police calls his running buddies.

My grandmother called me Bunk, because that's what my grandfather called me.

For her, the nickname Bunk meant the two of them taking their three-year-old grandson to the sparkling new Glen Burnie Mall for strawberry milkshakes.

It meant better days.

My grandmother tended to have her own view of things.

In my first year of Little League, I struck out thirty-one straight times.

And she kept telling me that all I needed was confidence.

Other people seemed to think I needed to swing at better pitches.

But my grandmother was fiercely loyal.

When I finally got a hit in my last at-bat of the season, she said, "See, I told you, Bunk, all you needed was confidence."

In her eyes, I never outgrew that loyalty—no matter how un-heroic the deeds.

In my third year at Virginia, I was the scorekeeper for the basketball team.

And we wound up playing Maryland in the semifinals of the ACC Tournament

For most of the year, we had been undefeated and ranked #1.

Early in the game, Lee Raker chased a loose ball out of bounds and knocked me half out of my chair. For a few seconds, the camera focused on the scorer's table while Lee picked me up and got back out on the court.

Of course, his hustle didn't do us much good. We lost by like 25.

Afterwards, everybody in Maryland—including my father—was gloating, because Buck Williams and the Terps had finally beaten Sampson and Virginia.

But, once again, my grandmother had her own view of things.

She called up my mother and said, "Did you see Dan on TV? I thought he looked good."

Mom-mom loved a party.

Weddings, birthdays—even wakes.

If she had been here last night, she surely would have said to everybody, "Doesn't she look good?"

She was proud of her Irish heritage.

And she did her best to live up to it.

She loved to laugh.

And she loved to talk.

And, whenever my father asked her if she wanted a Highball, she'd say, "Well, okay, John. But not too strong."

Those of you who've had one of my father's Highballs may be surprised that she never sent one back.

If you saw the picture collage on the DVD last night, you may remember a black and white photo that my father took at some birthday party on Beechfield Avenue.

With a cup of coffee raised halfway to her lips, and waving a cigarette in her left hand, my grandmother holds court.

She is a picture of vibrant, post-war prosperity.

That was my grandparents' moment: a time when everybody smoked and drank and listened to Sinatra.

It was a moment they thought would last forever.

And, like the glory days of the Rat Pack, my grandparents' moment was gone—stolen from them—before they turned around.

But, for better or worse, my grandmother never let go.

She lived for the memory of those days.

Though she endured great sadness, today is not a sad occasion.

On a recent visit to St. Elizabeth's, Sarah and I took along our granddaughter, Tayler.

To my grandmother, seeing Tayler nose around the room was an occasion for joy.

And seeing me take Tayler in my arms was proof of forty-two years devotion to the memory of my grandfather.

If you believe that great devotion earns its reward, then today is a time for celebration.

It's a time to celebrate, because—after half a lifetime—Dots is back with Bud, the way she always wanted. And always believed she would be.

Indulge Yourself
By Dan Peightel
(book recommendation)

Even if you've never cared about the distinction between sensuous and sensual, you owe it to yourself to luxuriate in Diane Ackerman's *A Natural History of the Senses*. Her prose is as rich yet subtle as Godiva chocolate, her surprises as exhilarating as a cool shower on a hundred-degree day. In the introduction, Ackerman hints at her organizing principle when she says, "The mind doesn't really dwell in the brain but travels the whole body on caravans of hormone and enzyme, busily making sense of the compound wonders we catalogue as touch, taste, smell, hearing, and vision." The book follows her senses, which she is unafraid to follow anywhere. In two pages about touch, for example, she connects Rembrandt to mirrors to language to Kafka to surgery, all to illustrate how we form our conception of a three-dimensional world. If you're tired of a puritanical routine with no room for "anything so unseemly as sensuous zest," treat yourself to a cream-filled pastry, a symphony, a massage, a slow deep wet kiss – all in one book.

Stories of Here and Now
By Dan Peightel
(book recommendation)

You may not know the name Richard Bausch. But readers a hundred years from now will. Each of the ten stories in his most recent collection, *The Fireman's Wife*, takes another step toward establishing Bausch as a rigorously unsentimental, yet deeply kind writer, as the Flaubert of our time and place. These stories, like his previous collection and four novels, recreate the day upon day of middle class American life, the quiet slippages between husbands and wives, parents and children. Sitting at a traffic light in the rain, Kenneth – the protagonist of "The Eyes of Love" – can no longer bear the argument he and his wife are having. "He looks at the green one two blocks away and discovers in himself the feeling that some momentous outcome hinges on that light staying green long enough for him to get through it." Reading these stories, you will recognize gestures you have used, tones you have heard, and you will suddenly know more about what went unspoken. You will understand, as Bausch does, the immense importance that can attach to something as meaningless as speeding safely through a traffic light.

Calling the Names of the Dead
By Dan Peightel
(book review)

Robert Kotlowitz opens *Before Their Time*, his memoir of World War II combat, with two two-page scenes that mark the unbridgeable gap between who he was and what the war made him. His story is nothing as simple and clean as another account of "the Good War" and "the Greatest Generation."

When Kotlowitz, a failing pre-med drafted "right out of the classroom" in 1943, leaves his family on the porch of their suburban Baltimore home, he believes in the war. "It seemed just and righteous to me," he writes. "In my simpleminded, adolescent way, I hated the Nazis."

Fourteen months later, stationed in a dilapidated Alsatian warehouse full of hungry rats and pools of dirty rainwater, he considers himself lucky. The straw he sleeps on smells of urine and cow dung. The soldiers he sleeps beside smell of sweat and soiled underwear. "But the underwear kept us warm when keeping warm was the point."

At first, the outlines of this story may seem familiar. But to fully understand the change wrought in Kotlowitz requires the memoir's careful unfolding of how and why he is assigned the duty of guarding that crowded warehouse of duffel bags belonging to the infantrymen of the 26th division.

Kotlowitz, whose first novel *Somewhere Else* won the National Jewish Book Award in 1972, circles back from his opening to introduce the officers and men of his unit. In brief sketches, he grants each man his full humanity – from Captain Antonovich, the ineffectual company commander, to Ira Fedderman, whose slovenliness and wheedling invite abuse.

The memoir follows Kotlowitz and his "buddies" from deadly maneuvers in Tennessee to dug-in positions near the Vosges foothills, each advance increasing the defensive silence between them. Their war culminates on a horseshoe-shaped ridge known as Bezange-la-petite.

Following hasty orders, they walk into an ambush that kills nearly forty of them, and forces the few survivors to play dead for twelve hours under heavy German fire.

Kotlowitz records the oozing of the sore that opens on his hip from lying on his canteen all that time. But he makes no attempt to impose a plot on the attack. This is not a movie, or even history. The ambush yields no heroism, only slaughter.

Most importantly, he refuses to sentimentalize the men of first squad, third platoon. As they lie in the mud, choking from thirst, Ira Fedderman dies "calling for his mother, the saddest call of all." But in that warehouse weeks later, Kotlowitz must call the roll of his dead comrades to another GI, who tosses their stenciled duffels from atop a pile. Fedderman's irregular bag hurts Kotlowitz's shoulder with its jagged edges. "I found myself cursing Ira Fedderman. Again. It never seemed to end. What in the hell could his personal effects amount to?"

Kotlowitz admits at the start to struggling with "the

passion to remember," to suffering "a small tremor of nervous agitation" at writing out the names. Such ironic understatement, even reticence, may conceal something of how he has lived with the "noise of Bezange" all these years. But calling out the names of names of the dead is never a lucky assignment.

To Boys Playing Soldiers at Pointe du Hoc
By Dan Peightel
(epitaph)

Spare, lads, thy sainted mothers' hearts.
Heed not orders from landed lords,
Nor siren songs of laureled death.
Heed instead the lone, anguished breath.

Until I Sign My Masterpiece
By Dan Peightel
(narrative description)

The cue ball thwacks the yellow ONE at the head of the nine-ball rack, splits the multicolored diamond like an atom. Balls clack toward all four rails, where entropy begins. Randomly, a slowing, clicking chain reaction spreads across the brushed emerald felt. With a goodbye kiss from the orange FIVE, the maroon SEVEN wobbles left toward a side pocket. A moment's hesitation. Then, thunk!

Surveying the table, I spot the problem ball, the purple FOUR, locked to the foot rail and guarded by the green SIX. I cut the ONE into a corner pocket and use the kick off the right side rail to draw the cue ball back toward the center of the table. The balanced cue feels like an extension of my fingers as I tap in the blue TWO. Then, flattening my bridge, I pocket the THREE. The backspin on the cue ball keeps it from following.

With no makeable shot, I play defense, knocking the FOUR from the rail. The crucial cue ball, loaded with running English, snakes behind the EIGHT. Seeing my opponent blocked, I think past sinking the FOUR to a possible FIVE-NINE combo for the win. Next time, maybe I'll run the table.

Where I Was When Elvis Died
By Dan Peightel
(memoir)

Some things you never forget. I was unloading tackling dummies from the back of a pickup truck. Even in dinnertime shade, dog day humidity added to the weight of the work. Coach Verbos, one of the new assistants, had heard the news on the radio as he carted the bags from the gym down to the practice field. Working in the truck bed, he pushed the blue bags onto the tailgate. I dragged them off the edge and hauled them into place for the drills.

"No way," I said.

"Yeah," he said. "Sounds like a heart attack."

"I remember when he did that satellite concert," I said, "*Aloha from Hawaii*."

I remembered the bejeweled costume. And the sweat. I meant that I'd barely given Elvis a thought since that 1973 made-for-TV special. The summer of '77 had been a long, steamy trek through misery and confusion. Five days before my seventeenth birthday, the news about Elvis was just one more sad, inevitable end, like finding Gatsby murdered, revolving on an air mattress in his own lavish pool.

But let me back up. The summer had started full of promise. I'd landed a job on the Saint Joe grounds crew. Brother Dominic drove us hard. But pushing a lawn mower around the 33-acre campus beat having to collect payment each month from the customers on my paper route. Instead of having to beg for my wages, I went to the Business Office like an adult and picked up my paycheck.

I filled the job's sweaty hours by daydreaming about my girlfriend, Betsy, and law school and the future we'd have together. Until the third Thursday in June, when we went to see *The Deep*. While Jacqueline Bissett, wearing only a bikini bottom and a white T-shirt, wrestled under water with vicious drug smugglers, I held Betsy's hand and squirmed in my seat and tried to hide how riveted I was.

On the way to Sorrento's for pizza, Betsy turned down a side street and parked under a shade tree. I slid toward her across the bench seat of her father's Nova. "We need to talk," she said. There was no reason, she said. It was nothing I had done. I said I hoped we could still be friends, asked if I could still call her, did everything but cry. Ten minutes later, standing at the curb outside my house, I dreaded going inside. I wanted anything but sympathy.

"You're home early," my mother said.

"I'm tired," I said. "I'm going to bed."

The next day, Brother Dominic sent the entire work crew down to the creek to pull football-sized rocks from the muddy bank and pitch them up onto the edge of the soccer field. Time never dragged slower for a prisoner on a chain gang. With each rock tossed I stood straight to ease my aching back and rub sweat from my eyes. And with each bend to dig another rock from the mud and weeds I imagined a different conversation with Betsy—

how I'd finally have my driver's license in a few weeks and everything would be better, how I'd hold off asking anyone else to my senior prom, how law school would mean a few years apart but after that we'd be happy and handsome and admired, how she was sorry for her terrible mistake and how I forgave her. But, trudging home, I couldn't think of what to say if her mother picked up the phone. So, after I showered, I tried to lose myself in a book.

Back in the first week of summer, on a library date with Betsy, the list of novels I had to read for AP English had seemed like a badge of honor. Now, I couldn't get past the first paragraph of *The Sound and the Fury*. "They took the flag out, and they were hitting. Then they put the flag back and they went to the table, and he hit and the other hit." And the opening of *A Farewell to Arms* felt just as daunting. "The trunks of the trees too were dusty and the leaves fell early that year and we saw the troops marching along the road and the dust rising and leaves, stirred by the breeze, falling and the soldiers marching and afterward the road bare and white except for the leaves." I did the math. Nine more weeks. And *Gatsby* was short. An extra week for *East of Eden*'s 600 pages. I had time. So I rolled over and went to sleep.

I woke up with poison ivy. It started with itching between my fingers. Soon, oily blisters covered my hands and arms, my neck and face, my forehead and around my eyes where I had wiped away sweat. Over the weekend, it spread to my torso and groin. Monday morning, I told my mother that I couldn't go to work. "You'll be just as miserable here as you will there," she said. It took half a bottle of calamine lotion. But, at five of seven, I sat in a shrinking patch of shade outside the Alexius Hall tool cellar waiting to punch in.

I also went to practice that night. Not because I was the reliable team manager. And not because the new head coach had promised to cut anybody who missed even one of the preseason practices to install the single wing. But because I wanted to see Betsy. Every Monday, she picked up her brother, Tommy, at the end of practice. In past weeks, there hadn't been much chance to talk, because I'd been busy stowing the medicine kit and equipment box and water bucket. But we'd always managed a smile and a wave.

That night, as the twilight faded to gray, I trembled when I spotted the avocado green Nova among the other arriving cars. If I headed to the gym right away on some important mission to the locker room, I might get to say hi in the parking lot. I hated how I looked, covered in calamine lotion. But then, suddenly, it didn't matter. Betsy's mother had come to pick up Tommy. As she drove past the baseball backstop up toward the gym, she looked straight ahead and gave no indication that she even saw me by the side of the road.

Later that week, pictures arrived in the mail from Betsy's junior prom, an 8x10, two 5x7s, and a sheet of wallet-sized prints. I stared at the girl in the portrait – creamy skin, sandy hair in a pixie cut, pretty toes in platform sandals peeking out from under the hem of her mint green gown. The guy beside her was a square-jawed unsung hero who would step forward in a crisis and bravely lead a crowd with just the right combination of words and actions. Or, he was except for the bent glasses, the wiry hair, and the throbbing zit on his chin.

My father's work schedule had delayed my taking my driver's test. So Betsy had driven us to the de Sales prom. After standing for the portrait, she spent most of the night in the ladies' room. And I spent most of it trying, through her friends Erin and Mary Beth, to convince her to come out and talk.

Despite what a miserable time it had been, I wanted to take the pictures to my room. "No," my mother said. "Leave 'em on the desk for Dad to look at." I hadn't told her yet that Betsy had broken up with me. She'd distrusted Betsy since the day of that library date, when she'd come home to find us alone in the kitchen, talking and sharing a Coke. I slapped the pictures on the desk. "There'll be other girls," she said. I didn't answer.

By the Fourth, my poison ivy had crusted over. All I wanted was to lie on the couch in the air-conditioned basement and listen to the drums and wails of Fleetwood Mac. For me, *Rumours* was the summer of '77 soundtrack. "Thunder only happens when it's raining / Players only love you when they're playing / Say . . . Women . . . They will come and they will go / When the rain washes you clean, you'll know. You will know." All I wanted was to soak in Stevie Nicks.

But my mother insisted that I go to Mom-mom's with her and Dad and Joe to eat hot dogs. We listened to the O's game over a transistor radio on the back porch.

Mark "the Bird" Fidrych pitched for the Tigers, with all his annoying antics—patting the dirt of the mound, talking to the ball. To get away from everyone, I went out through the basement and down to my grandfather's dogwood tree by the alley fence. But Mom-mom kept talking and laughing with Miss Catherine, her neighbor on one side, and Mister Gary and Miss Shirley on the other.

The only refuge was the tiny restroom in the basement, just a knotty pine closet with a toilet and a sink. I took the Salvadore's Gulf Station calendar hanging inside the door and paged back to the night of that first, slow dance. February 11th. The Valentine's Mixer in the gym. The Eagles. "Take It to the Limit." Four months together. We rode all around Catonsville that first night, dropping off her bevy of friends. By the time we doubled back to my house, only Mary Beth remained as chaperone. Betsy and I kissed good night, while Mary Beth giggled and froze out on the curb. One hundred twenty-six days.

The calendar back on its nail, I washed my hands. Attached to the base of the mirror behind the sink was a powder blue cardboard strip with red lettering. "Smile! You're on Candid Camera!" I could hear my grandparents, at their famous basement parties, guffawing with their friends over the lame, Allen Funt gag. My grandfather had been dead almost thirteen years. But the wilting sign still hung there by rusting thumb tacks, one more museum piece my grandmother couldn't part with, like his wrenches and screwdrivers hanging in precise rows on the pegboard above the workbench.

In the following weeks, Brother Dominic forgot about the rocks pulled from the creek. The crew spent long, blazing afternoons on the football field, raking off straw laid in the spring to cover new seed. Minutes crept like hours. And, at home, four books lay unread. I picked up the one I had a chance to finish before the test on the first day of school.

Wanting to be rid of Betsy, and unable to forget her for even a moment, I somehow lost myself in *Gatsby*, racing at breathless, breakneck speed through a sweltering, fatal Sunday. So many readings later, it's difficult to recreate that first rush of turning pages and unfolding plot. "The 'death car,' as the newspapers called it, didn't stop; it came out of the gathering darkness, wavered tragically for a moment and then disappeared around the next bend." Gatsby's dream feels so close that we can almost touch it. And then it's gone.

The denouement is inexorable. Weeks before his death, Gatsby fires his servants and replaces them with associates of the gangster Meyer Wolfshiem. The new chauffeur hears the shots. But "afterward he could only say that he hadn't thought anything much of them." Only the narrator, Nick Carraway, "rushing anxiously up the front steps," raises an alarm. But, like Nick and the three servants who hurry down to the pool, we already know.

And so it was with Elvis. We already knew—or thought we knew—"what preyed on" him, "what foul dust floated in the wake of his dreams." We were sure the hangers on who found him dead in a bathroom of his Graceland mansion cared as little about him as

Wolfshiem's people cared about Gatsby. Hungry as all the others for gossip about the King, we later heard or read somewhere that they found him face down in his own vomit, his gold silk pajama bottoms around his ankles.

Some things you never forget. Even when they have no real connection to you. Coach Verbos was a barrel-chested, jowly guy, a dentist with bad five o'clock shadow. Except for those few minutes on that one night, our interaction was always him giving me instructions. Close to forty years old, he had undoubtedly come of age listening to Elvis. But, that night, on the edge of seventeen, I couldn't see how the news about Elvis's death might have forced him to face his own mortality.

Nor could I see much of anything else. I couldn't see how pulling computer cable and fighting traffic back and forth to D.C. wore on my father. Or how my mother worried over all that could happen on a given day. I couldn't see that my brother, three years younger than I was, wanted to pursue art rather than sports. Or that my grandmother's devotion to my grandfather meant a devotion to widowhood. I couldn't even see Betsy, except as the object of my dreams.

Years and books and real disappointments later, I acquired a taste for Hemingway and Steinbeck and Faulkner. But, in the summer of '77, besides Stevie Nicks, only Fitzgerald spoke to me. Like Gatsby, I chased after "the green light, the orgastic future." Of course, Elvis knew. Our crystal visions, like a heartbeat, drive us mad. Year by year they recede before us. That painful summer, down at the end of Lonely Street, I found my own place to dwell.

Where Peace and Justice Must Begin
By Dan Peightel
(personal essay)

When the Archdiocese "clustered" St. Joseph's Monastery with three other parish schools and sent us to Madonna Middle for eighth grade, Miss Benner came with us. I thought that meant she'd look out for us. But the first day in the old St. Benedict's building she mixed us in with all the other kids, four desks to a "table."

I got stuck with Martha Durkin and two kids from St. Jerome, the school from Pigtown that the Archdiocese had closed. The girl catty-corner from me, Teresa Getty, never looked up from her desk. The boy to my right, Stephen Mealey, answered in a whisper when Miss Benner called his name. They both suffered from bad, purple acne splotches.

At recess, my Monastery friends told me that the St. Benedict's kids said Teresa was "a real skag," and Stephen was "a real fag." Somebody branded him "Feely Mealey." Everybody said I'd better not let him get too close to me, or he might try to feel me up. There was no way I was going to let him get close to me, whether he wanted to feel me up or not.

I came to school that September with a broken collarbone. So I watched lunch-time football from the sidelines, just like Stephen. He stood over by the rectory, his left arm crossed behind his back, his hand clasping his right arm just above the elbow. He never once made a move toward my spot by the fence. "He even stands like a faggot," somebody said after lunch.

$$****$$

Miss Benner never preached her politics to us. She just lived them. She wore clogs and baby doll dresses, rings on three fingers and bangle bracelets. When she got excited at the board, collecting the words and ideas we called out, her long brown hair flew from side to side. Nothing got rejected out of hand. Everything was possible in a first draft.

Although she never said so, I knew she was against the war and detested Nixon. When I found out that she listened to Simon and Garfunkel, I wanted her to know that my father did too. And I tried to write pieces that showed her I knew what was going on in the world.

One Saturday, I scribbled a story about a wounded Confederate soldier, "only a boy of 19 years." Lying in a hospital after having his arm amputated, he wonders, "What have I got against a Yank? I've never seen one except looking down a bayonet." The Rebel soldier survives, but he remains troubled long afterward. The story's final paragraph culminates with his dying thought. "Maybe this is the greatest tragedy of war: the warriors don't really know the people whom they are fighting."

The Vietnam War barely touched my suburban childhood. Could I really have known then, just from the pictures on the evening news, how little we understood of the Vietnamese we killed? All I remember thinking about were the American boys who were dying. It would be years before I read about Vietnam and its ancient civilization.

About a week after I gave the story to Miss Benner, she called me aside on the playground and told me that Father Stephen, the pastor, had pointed out something to her. The best thing about the story, he said, was how it started out objectively, then went inside the thoughts of the main character. Using my own story, she explained point of view to me. After I reread it, I never read as childishly again.

*****

"Frogging" somebody meant punching his thigh with a fist sharpened by the curled knuckle of your middle finger. One good "frog" could leave a bruise that would last for days.

I don't remember who first said, "Hey, let's all frog Mealey." Or how many people actually punched him. I'm glad I wasn't one of them. At least I have that.

But I watched. I knew it was wrong. And I did nothing.

Darryl Lynch finally stopped it. Not to keep from getting in trouble, I think now—though that's how he acted at the time. But because he recognized unfairness.

Back in homeroom after lunch, I told Stephen they didn't mean anything by it. I wanted to keep him from telling on us.

His eyes glistened with tears. His jaw muscles twitched. Lifting his desktop to hide for a moment, he wiped his eyes once with his finger. But he never made a sound.

The next morning, before school, Miss Benner asked me to come downstairs with her. I thought she wanted to talk about my new story on nuclear war between Russia and China. She took a piece of mail to the office. On the way back upstairs, she asked me whether I knew if anything was bothering Stephen Mealey.

"No," I said. "Not that I know of."

"Are you sure?"

"Let me think," I said. Pale yellow sunlight filled the stairwell. I squirmed in her silence. "No, I can't think of anything."

As we reached the half-landing, she said, "Okay, if you're sure." Then she paused on the stairs. "Because we have to speak up about things that are wrong," she said. "Even when it's hard. People who cover up for other people are just as guilty as those who commit the crime."

No one ever got in trouble for frogging Stephen Mealey. Maybe he convinced his parents that it would be worse to make a big deal of it. Or maybe Miss Benner was only guessing that morning.

She wrote on my final report card, "It was enjoyable teaching Danny. I hope he continues his interest in creative writing, as well as his belief in the ideals of peace & justice." I wonder how much irony she intended.

On the night we graduated, with all the girls in short summer dresses, I hardly noticed Stephen Mealey. And I've never seen or spoken to him since. But I've never forgotten one of the sins for which I need to be forgiven.

The Pose That Love Remembers
By Dan Peightel
(personal essay)

In the summer of 1958, two years before I was born, my father wanted a week away from the demands of his branch service manager, who wrote in his performance review "tends to be tardy." My mother, who typed the official copy of that review, wanted a week away from the bickering between the spinster who once ran the office and the new boss, whose petty dictates drove the old woman to distraction. But, most of all, John Peightel and Marie Ernest wanted to be with each other.

"Just day trips," she says. "Nothing special." Even if her father would have allowed anything else, day trips were all the young couple could afford. The week before, in her parents' cramped kitchen on Beechfield Avenue, after scraping together the last payment he owed to S&N Katz, John gave Marie the ring they'd picked out back in January.

He knew that she loved the operatic singing of Mario Lanza. And that while she was bedridden with rheumatic fever in second grade a friend of her grandmother's sat on and cracked her favorite record— Gene Autry singing "Back in the Saddle." In eight months of dating, of letting her fill the awkward silences, he'd picked up tidbits, glimpses that charmed him.

About him, skinny and crew-cut, with horn-rimmed glasses and a strong, jutting chin, she knew mostly that he worked hard, and that he wanted to marry her and start a family. She understood his silences as just the awkwardness of love. She didn't know yet that no one from his family would attend their Catholic wedding, or that it would take her a lifetime to learn all the moods of his silences.

On Tuesday of their week together, they rode up to Gettysburg. He drove, of course, in his tan and brown, 1953 Studebaker. They listened to Perry Como's "Catch a Falling Star" on the radio, and to Peggy Lee's "Fever," which he dug and she found monotonous. They clucked over the Liz Taylor, Eddie Fisher, Debbie Reynolds love triangle. And, to pass the time, they clucked about coworkers and friends.

When Marie had dropped out of Towson State Teachers' College in October of '56, her high school classmate Dolores Lolli had recommended her for the job at Burroughs. After work every Thursday, Marie and Dolores took the Number 3 down to Hutzler's and Hoschild-Kohn to spend the leftover part of their paychecks—the part they didn't pay to their fathers for room and board—on shoes and skirts and earrings. One day, in the late summer of '57, Dolores came into the office wearing a full, flared black and white skirt that caught John's eye.

"He asked if he could take her picture sometime," Marie says. "And, oh, she was flattered." He also asked if Dolores thought Marie would like to come along, because he had this friend, Jack Roberts. The Sunday afternoon date yielded the desired picture, but that was all. Or almost all. "After that," Marie says, "John asked me out."

He liked that she was smart without needing to show it, without needing to talk every minute.

On the way to Gettysburg, John and Marie stopped to see a shrine to Mother Seton, the patroness of Marie's high school. He spotted the bench in the dappled shade of the willow tree. "Here," he said. "Sit over here." He photographed her in several different poses. Then he had her turn slightly to the side and curl her right leg under. And he gave her a willow leaf that he picked from the ground. She held it up with her left hand, unconsciously showing off her ring. "Just like that," he said.

He knelt before her, adjusting focus with what seemed to her adoration. For him, the choice of angle was a matter of craft, a technique learned from reading *Popular Photography* and studying the glamour work of Paul Gowland. The rising line formed by the dark hem of the skirt would draw viewers to her lustrous eyes. "Tilt your head a little," he said. "To the right."

And just before he pressed the shutter he coaxed her smile. "Look at the camera like you're in love." She gazed into the lens—gazed at him—with a smile both patient and expectant, a smile that promised understanding. At that moment, she couldn't imagine that love would ever change, that there would be times, over the course of a life together, that she wouldn't want to pose just so.

On a January morning, a Wednesday, not quite seven years later, when it felt like she had the life Dolores Lolli and every other Seton girl wanted, a devoted husband and two healthy boys, Marie's father would die of a heart attack. Her dreams shrank that day. If her father had lived longer, she almost certainly wouldn't have lived her life paralyzed with fear behind the wheel of a car. If her father had lived longer, my parents almost certainly would have left behind their two-story row house in Beechfield for a rancher in the county.

Over the years, my father has photographed my mother in front of every Christmas tree, on every vacation and cruise, at every birthday and graduation of both sons and every grandchild. Occasionally he has caught her unguarded. More often, her smile seems embarrassed and artificial, a mask for her cares, her nagging worry about what might happen.

In 1969, around the time of their tenth anniversary, my father hung a framed print of the willow portrait on the knotty pine wall next to his cluttered workbench. As a kid, I hardly noticed the picture, took it for granted, just as I did that my mother would be there when I came home from playing ball. Only now am I beginning to understand that, through arthritis and arguments about wall paper, through worries about tuition and worries about retirement, through all the poses of love that a marriage requires, my father still remembers who my mother is.

The Price of Respect
By Dan Peightel
(memoir)

Rather than the black habit, crucifix, and dangling chaplet of an older generation of Xaverians, Brother Brian Vetter, my teacher for Honors Freshman English, wore striped shirts and plain polyester ties. *The Quill* had just run a picture of him in muddy sweats at a charity flag football marathon. But now, with his sleeves rolled up, and thin strands of hair combed across his balding head, he glowered from behind his raised desk.

"It might be in here," I said, opening an olive-green, hardcover edition of *Word Wealth*. As fast as I could, I unfolded every scrap of paper that I had stuffed between the pages—some corrected German homework, a mimeographed West Civ handout, three or four poor algebra quizzes.

"Are maybe not," Brother said. Even in mid-October, it still took me a moment to recognize his pronunciation of the word *or*. His scowl turned into a condescending grin. "Maybe you should come back after skull."

Did that mean I should or shouldn't? He talked in riddles. I wished that I were back in English class at the Monastery, where Miss Benner encouraged us to write poems and collect homonyms.

At St. Joe, the teachers were men, stern men. In the second week, Brother Corby, the gigantic, black-robed Dean of Students, had lifted a sophomore off the floor by his sideburns and pinned him against a locker until he gave up the guys loitering at the smoking shed. The teachers were men. And I was nobody.

Brother Brian, after giving the other guys a head start on a packet of grammar exercises, turned back to me. "What are you waiting for?" At the end of class, he took the late vocabulary assignment from me without a word. I left determined to do better.

Second semester, Brother eased up some, letting us read a novel of our own choosing. When he called me up to his desk, I hoped he'd be impressed with my choice, *The Fires of Spring*. My father had said it was Michener's best book. But Brother read the mass-market blurbs on the back and laughed. "It's fluff," he said. "But, okay, I guess."

One afternoon in late March, Brother captivated some of us by summarizing just enough of *The Lord of the Rings*. Near the end of that class, I told him that I was sure my father had read it. He grinned and said that he doubted that. His tone made me want to prove him wrong. I went home and searched every bookcase. Maybe he had said *Theirs Was the Kingdom*. R.F. Delderfield. J.R.R. Tolkein. Two or three times I paged through Delderfield's novel about the British Raj, but I found nothing like the tale of wizards and destruction that Brother had described.

I wanted to buy everything Tolkein had written. My mother said I could start with *The Hobbit*. Sixty pages in, I bogged down amid the geography of Middle Earth and the differences between trolls and orcs. Reluctantly,

Brother Brian let me switch books. I finished the year reading *QB VII*, a semi-historical novel about British courts and the Holocaust. Like my father, the author, Leon Uris, had attended high school at Baltimore's City College. My father bragged about that. But I never told Brother Brian.

Over the next three years, I saw Brother mostly in the gym. I was head manager of the varsity football, basketball, and baseball teams. He coached cross country, wrestling, and track. Sometimes in the equipment room, he would ask what I thought of some current event or cultural trend. Usually, he would walk away shaking his head, muttering in dissatisfaction. Once, I denied being a fan of *Charlie's Angels*, and I could tell from his grin that he didn't believe me. Even senior year, when I took AP English with Mr. Bauernschub, Brother never gave any indication that he thought I had distinguished myself. But a few years later, when I came back for a job interview, he remembered, enthusiastically, that I had been a National Merit semi-finalist.

In my first year as a teacher, he was the Dean of Students. Citing "the latest research on enabling," he banned student smoking on campus that year—and endured the grumbling of those used to confusing a privilege with a right. Unlike Brother Corby, Brother Brian never resorted to corporal punishment. But he commanded every bit as much fear. Adopting the face of the job, he would appear, unsmiling, in a doorway, and the room would fall silent. He strove not to be liked, but to be respected. And he was, even by the worst JUG kids.

After his stint as Dean, students saw a different side

of him. He served seven more years at Saint Joe, as a counselor in the Guidance Department. Then, in 1992, with a good deal of reluctance and barely a word of Spanish, he left the Mount for Bolivia, because that's where the Xaverian Brothers needed him to serve God. In his new post, he ministered to street children in Cochabamba, to kids so poor and troubled that they needed lessons in basic hygiene before they could attend school. Bolivia became Brother's home. He lived there almost as long as the 22 years he spent at the Mount. For a while, it seemed that Brother would never return to the United States. But in 2017 he came did come back, and he now ministers to immigrants in El Paso, Texas.

I think of Brother Brian whenever some Honors Freshman shows no reaction to a possibility that I see in his work. At fourteen, I overestimated how much Brother cared about a missed homework. I had only an immature notion of what it meant to think for myself. And I had no idea of the price that teachers must sometimes pay for the good of their students. Now, when many of my freshmen still secretly hope to believe everything they've heard from their fathers, I pray for the courage to risk not being liked.

Thinking, Digitally
By Dan Peightel
(cultural observation)

Eighteen months ago, soon after I bought my iPhone 4, I bought a book about how to use it. "Dude," my brother said. "You've got to learn to think digitally." With three screen taps (Safari—Bookmarks—iPhone User Guide), he had free at his fingertips everything for which I had schlepped to Barnes & Noble and paid $24.95.

Since then, while learning the rudiments of Facebook, Blogger, Twitter, and Edmodo, I have downloaded three e-books—each an exploration of teaching and learning; each through a one-click order—from Amazon to the Kindle app on my iPad. And I have thought hard about what it means to think digitally.

The commercials, of course, for the iPad Mini or Windows 8 or whatever, want us to believe that it means we'll never have to think again, that the machines will let us do all we've ever wished we could—paint like Monet, play piano with one finger, explore the heavens. The ads promise a world that will bend to the whims of a troupe of teenagers dancing with their convertible laptops.

The techno wizards have conjured the greatest marketing dodge since extra chrome on Cadillacs. To disguise their schemes of planned obsolescence, they sell the dream of perpetual ease. All you need is the latest device. And an unlimited data plan.

"I'm Billy Pierce," the shy kid tells us. "And I gave Charlotte back the stars." Click, click, click, and the nerd has won the heart of the girl next door. Never mind that he first speaks to her only after she moves to another state.

"Google, how far is the earth to the moon?" a little girl asks. And, instantly, the doting computer answers her. Finding what we want is so simple a child can do it. Never mind that the little girl's question is ungrammatical. No one even has to read directions.

Our experience, however, fails to match up. The wonders are too often contingent. A new, expensive wireless printer works with our laptop, but not with AirPrint for iPad. Edline opens on the iPad, but GradeQuick won't, so we're still bound to our desktops when sending attendance to the school office. Edmodo offers me "easy ways to post quizzes, polls, alerts, and assignments," but nothing for the one thing that would really save me time. Every two weeks, I still have to sort student captions and type contest ballots by hand.

Despite such frustrations, I know that I cannot ignore the digital revolution. Massive online open courses (MOOCs) have already begun to change higher education. How long can it be before iGeneration high schoolers and their parents, accustomed to personalized, on-demand selection of books, music, movies, news, TV shows, and more, will insist on (or create) the same flexibility in meeting their learning needs? In *Disrupting Class: How Disruptive Innovation Will Change the Way the World Learns*, a trio of professors from the Harvard School of Business predicts that by 2019 half of all high school courses in the United States will be taught online.

But my doomed effort to keep pace with digital technology comes from more than my instinct for survival. I see a chance to improve my teaching. That chance, however, depends on knowing enough to help my students use technology as a tool for discovery. Take Twitter for example.

Without question, Twitter users communicate in ways that are unfamiliar to me. But I believe my students who tweet want to be heard. If I can learn to use hashtags, maybe I can engage those students in a conversation about when and how any of us understand each other, or make ourselves understood. And, who knows? If one of them retweets a memorable heroic couplet, maybe proverbs or prophecies or epitaphs will start trending.

Much that's tweeted is shallow, or worse. But the same is true of much that's been printed since Gutenberg displaced illuminated manuscripts with vernacular translations of the Bible. The price of the Renaissance, Shakespeare, and the Enlightenment was a lot of rude speech and disturbing ideas. Use of Twitter's shorthand doesn't require us to abandon standard written English. It allows us, like every generation before us, to reinvent language by using it anew. Tweets are neither good nor bad, but thinking makes them so.

Of course, by the time you read this, Twitter's moment may well have passed. My larger point involves helping students make connections, helping them demonstrate what they know through what they can produce. I imagine a future where students and teachers collaborate in multi-disciplinary computer simulations that help students see the effects of their choices.

A large-scale model for this type of project already exists in the UVa bay game, developed by a faculty and student team at the University of Virginia. According to the game's website, it has "166 live players" studying the Chesapeake Bay through a simulation that "combines a video-game format with current demographic, economic, and scientific data."

The creation of such a game undoubtedly benefits from the funding and resources available to a major university. But, on a smaller scale, I can imagine a high school robotics class building a submersible that wins a competition at the United States Naval Academy, or a programming class writing code whose instructions are tested aboard the international space station. Wait, I don't have to imagine these classes. Mr Kapusinski already teaches them.

Let me imagine then a digital archive called *Timepieces* that begins with inquiry into the stories suggested by family photos. To construct the history missing from mute photographs, students would collect and curate digital copies of artifacts such as letters and diaries, newspaper clippings, magazine ads, and notes from family Bibles. All of their captions and interviews and analyses, covering events as varied as Civil Rights protests and Super Bowls, would be stored in the cloud and manipulated and edited and shared online.

No matter how powerful their search engines, students will always need to form critical questions.

Educational bureaucrats and textbook publishers may dream of online mega-courses that improve economies of scale. But I imagine computers helping me challenge every student every day.

Training Tales: Class War
By Doug Lambdin
Published in *Education Week Teacher Magazine*
(memoir)

Three years ago, at age 29, I took my first teaching job. The principal explained that I would be working with emotionally disturbed high school students who could "get a little out of hand." She assured me that an upcoming three-day training session would give me all the tools I needed to handle them.

On the first day, 14 of us filed into a windowless conference room on the bottom floor of the school. We were all dressed comfortably, as had been suggested, and we arrived with pads and pens. We wouldn't take any notes, however. Our instructor, who moonlighted as a bouncer, devoted the three days to what he called "hands-on" training.

Covering the floor of the room was a patchwork of blue vinyl mats, the kind used for teaching tumbling and gymnastics in PE. After splitting us into two groups (men and women), the instructor schooled and tested us in techniques to escape from choke holds, hair pulling, and biting. We were also taught to administer restraints, either singly or as a team. The instructor explained that students who are out of control—in danger of hurting themselves, someone else, or valuable property— need to be restrained on the floor until they're "back in control."

By the end of the first day, our legs were so sore that climbing flights of stairs required several breaks. But what bothered me more was that I wanted to teach— not engage in jungle warfare. After the training, I swore that I would never use what I had learned. Regretfully, it was the most useful training I've ever had.

My Father's People
By Dan Peightel
(family reflection)

Slouching in the backseat of the family Nash,
Mickey wishes that they could stop to take the pictures he
frames through the driver's side window—a copse of
trees beside a bend in a creek, a slanted basketball hoop
nailed to a weathered barn, a scalloped metal chair
rusting on a roadside porch. But his father, Amos, drives
with stoic resolve. Except for red lights, and once to put
water in the radiator, they won't stop until they reach
Washington Monument State Park, where they always eat
lunch on their way to Hagerstown.

Having bickered earlier about window seat and
middle, the twins, Connie and Carol Anne, ride beside
Mickey in stony silence. Up front, their mother, Thelma,
holds Terry on her lap. Eight-year-old Angela, wedged
between her parents, points out moo cows to amuse her
baby brother. Mickey knows almost nothing about his
parents' lives, the history of tones between them.

He vaguely remembers a house with a maid on
Potomac Street in Hagerstown, back before '41, before
they moved to Baltimore, to the rented house on Charles
Street, where his mother treks to the basement herself
and shovels coal into the furnace. His father endures
Easter and Mothers' Day visits to Anna Mae Allen, the
woman who raised Thelma and who Mickey remembers
living with for a year, endures these forced-smile

reminders of better days and his failures.

During the drive, Mickey thinks about Sue Vlegas and Eleanor Munn, girls from the Lovely Lane Methodist Church. What will they think tonight when he isn't at the MYF party to take their pictures? His mother has warned him that they count themselves too good for him. The bluntness of her words suggests to him that she thinks they're right.

As soon as his father parks, Mickey wanders, camera in hand, to the edges of the picnic site, looking for valley views and the play of light through the May leaves. When he turns back, his parents and sisters and brother have forgotten his camera. He sees them as they are, people busy with the struggle of living, people in the midst of rolling a cigarette, swigging a Coke, unpacking bologna sandwiches and pickles and a tin of homemade fried chicken, separate people, thrown together by the accident of family, tied by the effort to love, but unsure of what they have to say to each other.

Mickey never introduces himself that way to his friends in the MYF. They know him as John. His first and middle names come from John Murphy, the man who introduced his parents to each other, a rare friend who visits the house on Charles Street. Mickey sometimes wonders why his parents don't call him by the name they chose. But he never asks. He accepts it as part of who they are.

A little more than six years after he takes the picture of their picnic lunch, he will become my father. Around that time, he will have to take his father's car keys away and, six years later, watch him die of emphysema.

Eleven years after that his mother will die of breast cancer. Within a year of her death, Terry will leave for Florida without a word and will not come back even for Angela's funeral. Connie will divorce and move to Boston. Carol will move with her husband to a cabin in the woods near Gettysburg. Each Christmas, Mickey sends gift-boxed cheese and hopes the phone call will be less awkward than the one the previous year. Though I have long known Mickey as Dad, I have barely understood his silences, barely known him at all.

Show, Not Tell
By Doug Lambdin
Published in *What Would Melvin Do?*
(reflection)

At just about the beginning of each new school year, I wish that I could travel back in time and re-teach my first students. I feel I did them a real disservice, and I would like right the wrongs of that year, applying all what I now know. Although I am not about to hunt down all 122 of them and send them hand written apologies, and although most have gone on to college and are flourishing in their careers and families, I still can't help fighting back the image of them sitting somewhere in front of a keyboard struggling to write a letter or an essay, fuming with frustration, and then cursing the name of their ninth grade English teacher as they conclude that it's all his fault. I realize that this wish isn't that uncommon among teachers, but it doesn't make it any less sincere.

What am I now doing differently? That's a book in and of itself. But if pressed, I'd have to say modeling. So much of what I originally did was lecture, chalk-talk, sage on the stage. Just tell them. And that does work with some, but not too many. What I neglected to recognize is how we actually learn best, through showing, not telling. It's like when someone says, Tell me a story. That's not what he's really asking. What he really wants is to be shown a story with words. We need the visual. We need the example. The proven pudding. Whether it's an essay or critical analysis or a poem, I give them the model and then we journey together toward the answer. It's no great secret that's the most effective way to learn. It's how I learned. It's how I've always learned best, through modeling, through example. And not just in the classroom, anywhere in life. Yet where I seemed to learn what has been most valuable to me is from the examples, the models, set by my father.

Recently on Facebook, a newly "confirmed" friend sent me a message that she recently remembered that my dad had taught her older sister to play guitar. He, too, was a teacher. A natural one. He had more different jobs than anyone I have ever known, but I mostly remember as a teacher. Not because he taught guitar and piano for so long, but because I can't ever recall him not teaching. It was a roll he was just suited for. However, I don't know how he would have fared in a classroom of two dozen adolescents. He could have handled the students, but he would have been confined by the four walls. His classroom was the world at large, and my sister and I were his chief pupils.

Unlike my teaching, my dad didn't make up lesson plans, create power points, and give quizzes. His teaching was conducted by the deeds he did, the words he spoke, and the actions he took. And I learned, constantly. My father never graduated high school because of his deafness and the need to help support his family. From time to time, that fact cropped up to alter his endeavors. Yet, Dad was an accomplished salesman, and he carried quite a respectable reputation. There was a certain company trying to recruit him for a lucrative position, which would mean a great deal more of much needed money. However, the policy of the company was that all sales personnel must have a high school diploma. Yet, he checked the box indicating that he hadn't graduated on the obligatory application. When he went on the interview, the vice president, who was pursuing him, reminded my dad of this. The VP's solution was to lie and check the box on the application next to "achieved high school diploma." For my father, that was out of the question. The VP all but begged my father, assuring him that it was just a formality, no one would ever know. My father never worked for that company.

I asked, "Why not just sign it? Who cares?"

My dad only said, "I try to live my life so nothing comes back to haunt me, especially some little lie on an application." My dad would never then turn to me and say, "Now you do likewise with your life's decisions." That was telling. Instead, he showed; that was teaching. It was because of those moments that my father had such a high reputation in a business where so many wished they hadn't forfeited their integrity, while my father fortified his. There were dozens of scenarios like these that I had heard, not just from him, but from so many others in his business who recounted them like folklore. No doubt about it; his example set a high standard to follow. And his was the one to follow.

It's why my father was a natural teacher—he modeled good, and he showed integrity and dignity, even to his last breath.

The final days of my dad's life was spent at home, in

hospice. The family sat with him around the clock and took care of him, as if he were a fragile newborn. More than once while I sat with him, he spoke out, "Jesus, forgive me. I know I have offended you." I first thought, If this man has offended Jesus, then I'm in real trouble. Moreover, this seemed like maybe it was a private thought, something between him and God. A confession.

Until his final breaths, my father kept his awareness. He knew who was sitting with him. He knew when I was there. He would open his eyes, look around, and then drift back into a light sleep. He spoke little, but what he spoke was very specific. He said he'd miss me. He whispered once that he thought I was a good son and a good father. And without hesitation I assured him that if any of that were true, it was only because of the examples he set before me.

And so as I sat there with him in those hours, it occurred to me that he was doing more than just bringing closure, saying goodbye, confessing even. He was still teaching. As he showed me how to live, he was showing me, in his final lesson, how to die. How to face the end. Setting one final example. Still, even then, he couldn't not teach, he couldn't not model, showing dignity, showing faith.

In writing about his own father, American writer Clarence B. Kelland remembers, "My father didn't tell me how to live; he lived and let me watch him do it." It is in that watching that we actually learn. The model that shows the way, whether it's in the classroom, in the work place, or in the final hours. Showing, not telling.

Made in the USA
Middletown, DE
01 August 2019